IMITATING AND FISHING
NATURAL FISH FOODS

IMITATING AND FISHING
NATURAL FISH FOODS

DAVE WHITLOCK

THE LYONS PRESS
Guilford, Connecticut
An imprint of The Globe Pequot Press

CONTENTS

LEFTY'S PREFACE

I first met Dave Whitlock several decades ago. This shy, but intense, young man introduced himself and explained that he was a scientist working in petroleum production. He hesitantly explained that he would like to get into the outdoor writing field, but was at a loss how to go about it. He asked me if I would help him. We sat down, and as we chatted over a few cups of coffee I realized here was someone who would be good for the outdoor field. I volunteered to do whatever I could to get him started.

Soon after Dave began his new outdoor writing career, he sent me a letter of thanks along with a box of flies. I still have that box of flies — every one of them made of deer hair! Of course, at the time, I had no clue of what a famous fly tyer and fly fisherman Dave would later become. But something kept me from ever fishing those flies. I felt that I should hold onto them in their original condition. I'm glad I did.

Over the years, Dave and I have grown to be the best of friends — almost like brothers — and there isn't anything in the world that I wouldn't do for him. I think he feels the same way about me.

Some of my finest memories have been of fishing the White and Norfork rivers with Dave. He opened my eyes to what fishing below dams could be like. Before that time I knew little about tailwater fishing. But it was when he introduced me to those huge Arkansas rainbows and browns that

I realized what a great all-season fishery a tailwater could be.

Over the years, Dave and I have shared many fishing trips and worked together as consultants for a number of tackle companies. We have also conducted numerous joint fly-fishing seminars for organizations such as Trout Unlimited and the Federation of Fly Fishers.

Dave is a superb angler. While most people have to work hard to develop their fishing skills, there are some people, like Dave, who are simply instinctive fishermen. If you put Dave on a piece of strange water, he seems to be able to master whatever new angling problems he is confronted with in very short order.

But, more than that, Dave has become one of our keenest observers of what trout (and all other freshwater species) eat—including why, how, and when their appetites are stimulated. *Imitating and Fishing Natural Fish Foods* is a good technical—but easy to understand—book that deals with freshwater fish foods and how they can be successfully imitated by fly fishermen.

At first glance, you may think you don't need the information contained in these pages. But let me assure you that an understanding of what Dave has put down on these pages in his words, photographs, and marvelous illustrations will make you a better fly fisherman.

I cherish the time and knowledge that Dave has shared with me. After you have finished reading this book, I think you will feel the same way, too.

Bernard "Lefty" Kreh
Hunt Valley, Maryland

INTRODUCTION

As man has evolved he has continually been linked with the water sources that are necessary for his survival. The waters of streams, lakes, and seas provide us with drinking water and the irrigation supply for our agriculture, as well as providing one of our major sources of foods that we gather or capture on lands adjacent to watersheds or in the water itself.

As a consequence, waters and the fish in them have become a major part of our lives and hold true fascination for us. Over the span of man's time on earth, in our attempts to catch fish for food we have developed many methods, from trapping, spearing, poisoning, and netting, to capturing them on poles with lines and hooks that are baited or dressed with objects fish are tempted to eat. All these methods have been greatly perfected as experience and technology have advanced our civilization. It is the pole, line, and hook method, however, that has evolved into one of man's most pleasurable activities. We call it *sport angling.*

Sport angling consists of either fishing with natural (organic) baits or fish foods, or fishing with artificial imitations of natural fish foods. And for this imitative sport angling, man has developed a huge variety of lures, plugs, spoons, jigs, and flies. All of these artificial baits and all of the various techniques for fishing them have their place and value in our recreational spectrum, but fishing with a fly has come to be recognized as the most intriguing, challenging, and respected

Natural Fish Food

way to outwit fish and to realize the most pleasure in the process of doing so.

The foundation of fly fishing from its beginnings centuries ago was constructed around the unique idea of matching the small insects that fish were observed to be feeding upon. Commonly these insect forms were called *flies*. Today fly fishing has evolved from just the imitation of insects to methods that are better able to imitate *all fish food forms* than any other type of sport angling, even including the use of live, natural baits or foods.

That fact creates the rationale for this book: to assist the fly fisherman first, to recognize all the foods that trout and other freshwater fish feed upon, and how and why and under what circumstances they feed upon them; and then, how to go about selecting artificial imitations of these foods and presenting them to the fish — fly fishing — correctly.

That might seem like a huge task for such a small book like this, since trout and other freshwater fish eat a wide variety of aquatic and terrestrial foods, feeding on literally thousands of food forms.

A True Feeding Frenzy

However, there are actually just a few basic groups of super foods that cover most of the foods fly fishermen need to imitate in order to catch those species of fish we consider to be most sporting on the fly.

Most freshwater fish that fly fishermen prefer to catch can be categorized as *predators* (fish who capture their food live) such as trout, bass, sunfish, pike, perch, and in some cases, salmon and striped bass. These predator fish feed on insects, fish, crustaceans, amphibians, reptiles, mammals, and various invertebrates, including aquatic worms, leeches, and snails. (As distinguished from *scavenger* fish, such as catfish, carp, eels, chub, and suckers, who will eat non-active or sluggish live animal foods as well as dead animals and hosts of aquatic and terrestrial plants and their fruits and seeds.)

Interestingly, all the predator fish, more or less, will feed on all types of live animal forms under certain circumstances. But while not exclusively trout foods (many other fish, such as perch, sunfish, and bass will also selectively or preferably feed on them) *insects, minnows* and *worms* are the three major food groups that trout prefer.

Predator Fish (Smallmouth Bass)

In this book I will be concentrating on a discussion of these major trout food groups and how they can be successfully imitated and fished with the fly. But even though I will be concentrating on trout, these observations can be readily adapted to fly fishing for any of the other freshwater species you wish to fish for.

The good news about these food preferences of trout is that there is never a stagnate situation in the world of the trout. Every day offers a new challenge to the fly fisherman to "match the hatch," especially so if you also tie your own flies. The only bored fly fishermen I ever encounter are those who dogmatically insist upon not offering the fish an appealing menu of flies that satisfies their hunger for the food they have decided to eat *that day*.

There is more or less a basic and natural common sense system to recognizing and identifying fish foods and imitating them with artificial forms or decoys. I like to think of these fake foods as sculptures made on fish hooks, in a manner that conforms with the design of a "fly" and that balances or works efficiently on fly tackle. The fly then needs to be cast to a fish and presented and animated realistically

Scavenger Fish (Channel Catfish)

or characteristically. The angler's deception continues until the fly is attacked and ingested sufficiently for its hook to penetrate and hold in the fish's flesh.

What seems to be the principal challenge of fly fishing with artificial imitations is that we are trying to confuse or fool one or more of a trout's food detecting senses (sight, sound, smell, touch, and taste) to interest it into capturing the fake long enough for us to strike and hook the fish. This is a special challenge not only to the angler, but also to the designer of the fly. And these challenges can sometimes come hours, days, months, or years before the fish is tempted by a particular fly. That is the what and why of this book. It is my task to prepare you to know what fish foods consist of so that you can prepare yourself to imitate them effectively as you encounter various fish feeding opportunities.

When I initially became interested in fly fishing, I was nine years old. The best way I can describe my thoughts at that time was that I was a "natural" naturalist. I was interested in all living animals and plants — especially those that existed closely beside, on, or in water. My keenest interest was to catch all types of aquatic creatures, but most especially fish!

When I was a very young boy, my parents and grandparents did an excellent job of teaching me their knowledge of how to fish with a net, spear, trout line, cane pole, limp line, and tackle. Most of their hooks were baited with live or very dead natural baits, and their artificials were large wooden and plastic lures which they called plugs. But by the time I was eight years old, I had more or less become dissatisfied with the tackle and artificials they were using. Looking back on those times, I can only explain my dissatisfaction by recalling that at that time, I was beginning to realize that there was a vast range of small natural fish foods in the water which were being eaten by some very nice fish — and we weren't catching them with my folks' methods!

Then I discovered fly fishing, and it seemed to hold the potential to imitate and animate *all food forms* — especially those very small delicate ones like aquatic and terrestrial insects, tiny fish, crustaceans, etc.

As I began to fly fish and mature into manhood, I sought to learn more about fish foods than I had observed as a boy. But I ran up against a solid wall of frustration in examining the fly-fishing literature of the 1940s and 1950s. I will just call it the "Latin Connection." The custom of that time — of using strange and unpronounceable Latin terminology to explain trout foods — confused, intimidated, and discouraged me so much that I turned away from trying to "book learn" fly fishing and fly tying.

Later, after I made contact with other beginners as well as experienced fly fishermen, I discovered that most of them, too, had been intimidated by the "Latin Connection" and had just detoured into sort of a generic type of fly fishing. That is, they would use just six or seven flies, which were generally an Adams, a Royal Wulff, a Gold-Ribbed Hare's Ear, a Gray Hackle Peacock, a Muddler, and a White Marabou Streamer or a Woolly Bugger. (Even today I still run across people who insist upon using only two flies, a Royal Wulff and a Woolly Bugger.)

Sure, we caught fish some of the time, but the fish were not the largest or smartest that were in the stream. And I can remember so many times seeing trout, bass, or panfish feeding wildly in front of me and I had no fly they seemed to want. Why? Because my limited knowledge and limited fly assortment could not match the appearance or behavior of the natural foods they were feeding on.

When I admitted this to myself I began to study again, but this time I used almost exclusively my powers of observation and common sense — plus a lot of *objectivity!*

If you were to observe just one pool on one stream for a year or even 10 years, you would discover, I think, that in the world of fish foods, exceptions are almost always the rule. Few constants exist. Consider then, thousands of watersheds across the 50 states that you might seek out to fly fish!

With this realization, you should attempt to master the basic facts about fish foods, allowing them to become your alphabet and vocabulary, which, when combined with current streamside observation, will allow you to construct a customized fishing procedure for *today*.

That is the purpose of this book: to make you more aware of fish food types, their why, where, and when; their importance as trout foods; how to choose and use fly patterns that will imitate them correctly, and it is hoped, successfully take fish after fish, all day long.

OVERLEAF: *Casting for landlocked salmon in Maine's Rangley Lake.*

CHAPTER ONE

FISH AND FISH FEEDING PERSPECTIVES

Just knowing what fish feed on is not enough to consistently catch them as they feed on those foods. I believe it is just as important to understand a fish's conception of its food. Before I begin describing the foods you should know about, I would like you to think about the following. Always try to consider what fish know about food, what times of day they are hungry, how they find food, how they acquire food, and the precautions they use to feed successfully without exposing themselves to harm or being eaten themselves.

Fish are classified as cold-blooded creatures. Unlike man, whose body temperature remains constant, body temperature of fish is approximately the same temperature as their watery environment. However, fish do have a preferred or optimum operational water temperature — a range in which they maintain their highest rates of metabolism and are the most active and alert. It is in this temperature range that they are most capable of finding, capturing, and digesting their foods. There are approximately four groups of fish species classified by their optimum operational temperature ranges:

Cold Water Fish (trout, salmon, char, grayling, striped bass) — 45 to 65 degrees F.

Cool Water Fish (whitefish, walleye, smallmouth bass, yellow perch, pike, pickerel, chub) — 55 to 75 degrees F.

Warm Water Fish (largemouth bass, bluegill, green sun-fish, crappie, catfish) — 60 to 80 degrees F.

Tropical Water Fish (all the tropical inshore and offshore saltwater species, peacock bass, southern largemouth bass, oscars) — 70 to 90 degrees F. (Excepting southern largemouth bass, most of these species will usually die in water colder than 50 degrees F.)

For all species, if you want to catch these fish, especially on imitations, fly fishing for them will be the most productive when the water is in the middle of these temperature ranges.

As the water gets colder by 10 to 20 degrees the fish become increasingly dormant-like. Their metabolism acts to slow down their bodies' functions, and they become slow, numbed and clumsy — in similar fashion to how your ungloved hands respond to very cold temperatures. At this time, because of this chilling effect, slower moving and smaller foods will have more appeal to the fish.

When water temperatures are warmer than the fishes' optimum operational zone, they will similarly become lethargic and disoriented, primarily because warmer water contains less oxygen which, in turn, affects the fishes' metabolism and threatens their lives. When you encounter such excessively warmer waters, look for areas where fish might find higher concentrations of oxygen. Such areas include the rapids in streams, riffles, or wind-blown surfaces. And in deep stillwaters, fish will swim and feed deeper where the water is cooler and contains more oxygen. In freshwater lakes, this area is usually referred to as the *thermocline*. In streams, the fish seeking cooler water for comfort and oxygen will also migrate to springs or seeping water sources if they are available.

Another consideration regarding water temperature is that in a watershed where the existing water is cold, such as in the winter and spring months, during the day fish will become more active as air and water temperatures are slowly rising, rather than falling, toward their optimum operational range. Conversely, in an existing warm-water temperature, such as in the summer and fall, fish will become more active when water temperatures are slowly falling.

Naturally residing fish-food forms, most of which are also cold blooded, are closely linked with these same optimum temperature ranges as are the fish. This is important to keep in mind: *more than any other stimuli, fish are much more often stimulated to feed by the increasing activities of their live foods.* For example, if a major hatch or emergence of mayflies occurs from, say, 9 a.m. to 12 p.m., trout will most likely be less active before 9 a.m. when the hatch commences, and less active after 12 p.m. after the hatch is over, even though the water temperature may be in their optimum operational range all day long. This is similar to the manner in which we adjust our bodies to create our keenest appetites at certain fixed times of the day.

Generally, the four seasons — winter, spring, summer and fall — will create operational temperature changes from too cold in the winter, to optimum in the spring, to too warm by mid-summer, to optimum by early fall.

Such seasonal changes will also cause fish to vary in location, mood, fitness, and aggressiveness. This behavior is especially pronounced just before, during, and just after spawning activity. At pre-spawn, most fish are feeding voraciously and are on the move. During spawn they tend to be very emotional, sometimes aggressive, combatant, territorial, and less interested in actually eating. After spawn they are in a weakened, stressed, post-natal condition and are also less apt to eat. But with the passage of time, they will gradually return to their normal daily feeding behavior.

Though fish are often easiest to catch during spawning season, fishing for them at that time is not the best sporting ethic, as they are more vulnerable, concentrated, and apt to fail at spawning or die if caught then. For this reason, many angling jurisdictions close their catch seasons during spawning. But even where it is not prohibited by law, the caring sports fisherman will refrain from fishing spawning areas. This is not only good sportsmanship; it is also good conservation practice to allow undisturbed time and space for the fish to complete their natural spawning activity.

FISH SENSES AND UNDERSTANDING HOW THEY USE THEM

SIGHT

Both predator and scavenger fish see well under and above water. They can see color and many detect subtle differences in color. But underwater visibility for a fish is restricted to how transparent the water is and how much light is available for visibility. If the water is colored (stained) or murky/cloudy with suspended particles, the fish cannot see any farther in it than you can. If a fly passes by them at a distance,

How a Fish Sees Through the Water's Surface

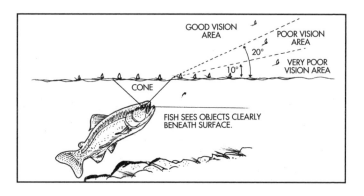

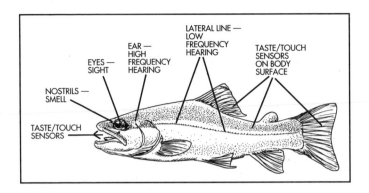

Fish Senses

say, of six feet, when visibility is limited to four feet, the fish cannot see it. So, to find it they have to rely on their senses of hearing or smell. Fish can only see above the surface at an angle or through a narrow cone of vision, due to light rays bending and reflecting off the surface.

Predator fish tend to use their sight more than scavenger fish to locate food. But both types of fish have their eyes advantageously positioned on their heads so as to provide them with a view of their most important food producing areas: above, in front, or below them, depending upon the species and its customary food forms.

HEARING

Fish hear underwater extremely well in two ways. One way is with the ears on their heads. This is much like how we perceive high frequency sound waves, as noise. A second method is by the lateral-line sensor running along their bodies which enables them to detect the very low frequency or pressure sound waves emitted by the movement of objects in the water. With these sensors, fish can easily sense an object moving toward or by them. In this manner, whether it be food or foe, the fish can determine the object's shape, size, speed and direction.

SMELL

Fish have a highly developed sense of smell, a sense that is often even more sensitive than that of a bird dog's ability to detect odors. Fish are attracted to natural food odors, but are generally repelled by human and petrochemical odors.

TOUCH/TASTE

Fish have touch/taste sensors on their bodies and mouths that are very sensitive in detecting real and fake foods. They usually use these senses for the final examination of a prospective food before they actually eat it. If you notice a fish strike at your fly, yet seemingly miss being hooked, it is probably because it touched and/or tasted the fly and immediately rejected it as soon as it was discovered to be unnatural.

PREDATOR FISH FEEDING BEHAVIOR

Predator fish usually capture and eat live, active foods such as insects, other fish, crustaceans, reptiles, amphibians and mammals. They do this using their senses of sight, hearing and smell mostly. Touch and taste are senses they use to decide if their captured food is edible. Keep this in mind. Because sight is usually the most important sense of predator fish, the *size, shape, action* and *color* of an imitation are the most important considerations to successfully imitating live food and deceiving fish. When their sight is handicapped or otherwise inhibited, predator fish must resort to their senses of hearing and smell (in that order) to detect food.

Daybreak on the Ozarks' White River. ➤

Predator fish prefer to conceal themselves in some manner to get closer to most live fish foods. They do this through camouflage, stealth, and concealment, which is specifically illustrated by their preference for feeding in low light levels common at night, twilight hours, and dark stormy days. There are also periods that coincide with "invertebrate drift," when many aquatic insect larval and nymphal forms expose themselves with a mass downstream movement. During high light intensity periods, predator fish will also use shade or water depth and color to reduce their visibility to their prey as well as to enemy predators.

Ambush and surprise are their main success factors. But swimming speed, such as that of the barracuda, or maneuverability, such as that of the bass, can also be very important contributors to feeding success for many species.

SCAVENGER FISH FEEDING BEHAVIOR

Scavenger fish will eat both inanimate foods and some live foods — just the opposite feeding preference to that of predator fish. Scavengers, however, should never be considered a less worthy sporting game than predator fish. They can often be more selective, spooky, and difficult to catch on artificials or imitations of their foods than predator fish. And they are usually strong and fast swimmers, often giving the angler a longer fight than will many species of predator fish.

Scavengers usually hunt and capture their foods through the use of their senses of sight, smell, taste, and hearing. And since many scavenger fish inhabit murky water or feed at night, their sense of smell is more important for locating food than is their sense of sight. I have encountered only a few situations in which I concluded that scavenger fish were using their sense of hearing to detect food. However, scavenger fish do constantly use hearing to detect and escape their predators. That is one reason why they are more difficult to present a fly to, and why they are often so difficult to catch. For example, to a much greater extent than predator fish, scavengers will scare easily when an angler causes wading, boating or casting noises in the water.

Since most scavenger foods are *inactive or slow moving* and are discovered by the fish by their senses of smell, sight, and taste, to enjoy a high percentage of takes on scavengers, I believe their imitative flies must be more realistic in shape, color, and texture than those required for predator fish. And it is very important that the fly fisherman present such scavenger food imitations accurately. Since scavengers feed very slowly and delicately (not much need for them to attack or kill their food), it is also important for the angler to see or precisely detect their soft, slow takes of fake food. That requires a lot of fly-fishing skill and total concentration.

CONCEPTS OF IMITATION

Fish food imitations may be grouped in four categories: *suggestive, impressionistic, imitative* and *exact imitative.* I am convinced that the flies that perform best for most fly fishermen in most waters are those that suggest or give the impression of a wide variety of foods that fish see the most often and prefer to eat. This is in contrast to the food imitations that approach anatomical perfection (exact imitation), whose effectiveness is narrowly restricted to just one food type.

This will also follow true if the fly fisherman is less than perfect in how he presents and fishes a particular fly. Say a nymph is presented and fished more like a minnow than a nymph. If a fish is selectively feeding on only nymphal forms, it will refuse to eat an object exhibiting minnow-like action.

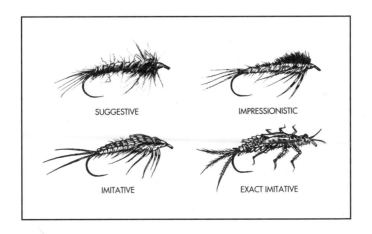

SUGGESTIVE

IMPRESSIONISTIC

IMITATIVE

EXACT IMITATIVE

Four Types of Imitation

But if the fish is after minnows, and the nymph imitation acts enough like a minnow, with minnow-like swimming actions, the fish may very well take it.

That's why the classic impressionistic flies such as the Gold-Ribbed Hare's Ear, the Woolly Bugger, the Muddler Minnow and the White Marabou Streamer have for years been successfully fished in many ways for nearly every species of predator and scavenger fish. All of these impressionistic patterns look and act like edible foods to most fish, whether the pattern is floating, sinking, swimming, crawling or sitting stationary on the surface of the water.

For the lesser-skilled fly fisherman, suggestive or impressionistic flies almost always catch more fish on the average than the really precise or exact food imitations. But as an angler's casting and manipulation skills increase — when he is able to correctly fish an imitative or exact imitative version of a fly — so does the likelihood increase that he will catch more and larger fish that are feeding selectively on a particular natural food form.

Because they are not imitations of fish food at all, I have not included them in the discussion above, but there is one other group of flies that needs mention: attractor or exciter flies. Salmon flies are in this group. Though not necessarily imitative of natural foods, they are often useful when fish are in non-feeding moods. Attractor type flies are usually highly visible, and may also be constructed to create lots of water action and emit sound vibrations that have proven to stimulate a positive response from some fish species.

There are even some odors that can be placed on these type flies to attract fish. Odor is a property of natural foods that fish really tune in on during much of their searching for natural foods. Yet scenting artificial flies that imitate a natural's odor is considered to be unethical or even illegal in most fly-fishing circles. There are arguments to be made on both sides of the question of whether or not it is ethical to scent flies. You'll just have to decide for yourself.

However, I do recommend that you at least *deodorize* a new fly to remove manmade odors which are often very offensive to fish. Do this by simply dipping the fly in the algae, moss, or mud of the watershed where you are planning to fish, and then rinse it well in the water. This simple and legal deodorizing procedure is usually accepted by even the most severe critics of fly scenting.

Similarly, after you have caught a fish, the fly will usually have become scented by the fish's slime, blood, etc. This is especially true of nymphs and other underwater flies. The odor that remains on such a used fly will definitely improve its attractiveness to your next fish. In fact, often the longer a fly is used the more effective it becomes. I believe this is because either contact with the first fish has served to deodorize manmade odors, or the fly's exposure to the local water environment has gradually scented it with odors that fish consider natural and appealing.

Fish definitely imprint on the foods they see and eat most often. Naturally, they prefer those foods that are most abundant and easiest to gather and eat — whether the food is pellets, worms, mayflies, minnows, or whatever.

The fish will often imprint so strongly on these foods that they will be selective to those foods and ignore or refuse other perfectly good natural foods. When this imprinted selectivity occurs, fish can be absolutely insistent that an imitation be exactly the same size, shape, color and have the natural's action — or they will refuse it.

More and more, because of the greatly increased fishing pressure we are experiencing on most of our waters, fish are learning to survive by being highly selective to a natural food. For example, this might mean that a trout living in a roadside Pennsylvania stream that is fished 10, 20, or 30 times a week might survive being caught and killed because it has been imprinted to eat only certain mayflies. These mayflies may be of a precise size, with legs, wings, and a tail action of a living insect that is in the act of emerging from its nymphal skin. If the trout were to violate this rule of natural selectivity — say to eat a larger, fuzzier, non-wiggling similar food — that may be the last food it ever eats!

Yet for some strange reason, I am always seeing fly fishermen who ignore this simple rule of natural selectivity. I'm not sure I really know the reason why.

Maybe it's because one of the peculiar characteristics of human behavior is our mistaken belief that everything bigger must always be better. Therefore, man is always trying to take everything he does to excessive limits. Whatever the reason, it is the root cause, I am convinced, that the two most common mistakes that are made by fly fishermen in imitating natural fish foods are as follows:

1) *Designing Flies of Excessive Size* — when we design our imitative fly patterns, we tend to make them larger or more bulky than is natural; and

2) *Fishing Them with Excessive Action* — when we manipulate our flies, we tend to impart excessive or unnatural movement to them.

So this point is worth repeating and emphasizing. There is a definite trend wild trout are moving toward: preferring smaller food forms and feeding more at night. This is because those trout that do survive today's increased angling pressure do so by being selective to smaller, harder-to-imitate food forms, for which the imitations are harder to fish properly; and by feeding more during the times when most fly fishermen have gone home. This behavioral change in the fish may be environmentally learned, but in my opinion, it may also be genetically linked.

In the following chapters, I will identify and describe fish foods for you as well as recommend imitations. As you read this material, keep in mind that to be effective in fly fishing with these imitative fly patterns, you must always be an objective observer of the entire environment in which the trout lives. The more you know about all the things that affect a fish's life, the better you will be at knowing that fish, and the better you will be at catching it. Your streamside observations and your common sense then need to be blended with your skills — first, to make the fish you cast to believe your imitation is real and safe to eat; and second, through the use of good technique, to put the fly where the fish can most conveniently find and catch it. These are the keys to success.

OVERLEAF: *Dave employs a stomach pump to find out what this trout has been eating.*

CHAPTER TWO

OBSERVING, COLLECTING, AND IDENTIFYING FISH FOODS

It is often said . . . and is so true . . . "There are never two days alike on a fishing water." That is because there are a host of daily variables in environmental conditions, including temperature, light, wind, precipitation, water level, water clarity, barometric pressure change, etc. And in response to these changes, since adaptation is an imperative of life-forms that survive, fish constantly alter their feeding behavior as such changes take place in their environment. Because of this, the most successful fly fishermen routinely make it their first order of business to find out the particular fish food preferences that are existing at the time they arrive at the water.

To effectively observe, collect, identify, and imitate fish foods, you need to have a good understanding of what foods fish prefer, and then determine if those foods are available in the watershed where you are fly fishing. Much of this principle you can master with your common sense and powers or "senses" of observation before and during the time you are fishing. *Look-Watch-Observe-React* is the first sense. *Listen-Hear-Consider-React* is the second sense. *Sample-Hold-Touch-React* is the third sense. Using these senses, you can discover what fish are feeding on, when they are feeding, how their natural foods are acting and reacting, and then apply that knowledge to making or purchasing imitations that will trick fish into thinking *your fly is what they want to eat.* That is the ultimate skill and thrill of fly fishing food imitations.

Here is what I do to observe, collect and identify the foods that fish are eating at any particular time.

OBSERVING FISH FOODS

Take five or 10 minutes before you start casting to thoughtfully examine the shoreline, the air above the water, the water surface, and the subsurface water column for fish food presence and activity.

Listen, Watch, and Focus — Tune into the whole wildlife scene and become a part of it. Listen for any wildlife activity: bird calls or songs, frogs croaking, crickets singing, hoppers clicking, flying insect swarms buzzing, and fish splashes. There is a music of positive wildlife activity when conditions are right, a silence when it is not. Look across the water, along it, above it, on it, and under it for the presence or absence of fish foods. Look for birds flying, herons hunting, insects flying and alighting. These are the neon signs that show and tell you what is "happening." I use and enjoy them all day, every day, that I fly fish.

COLLECTING FISH FOODS

It is a good idea to get a close-up look at the possible foods available. A close approach or binoculars help tremendously, but if possible, I like to capture a few actual fish food samples using a variety of instruments — a fine mesh aquarium net, a small mesh hand seine, a fly swatter, or what have you — rather than just my bare hands.

Stomach pump contents from a trout show exactly what foods the fish has recently preferred.

As I fish I continue to watch for fish foods and collect more samples if I run across foods I am unfamiliar with. I watch closely what the fish are attempting to eat. It is also a good idea to check out what fish have actually eaten as you catch them. I do this by looking in their throats, feeling their stomachs, or pumping samples out of their stomachs with a simple, harmless stomach pump before releasing them.

If you kill your catch to eat, be sure to autopsy its stomach for food contents. This can give you valuable, precise information on exactly what food fish are feeding on.

It is also a good procedure to collect and preserve these food samples to aid in identification and imitation when you return to your lodging at the end of the day, either for your own use (if you are fly tyer) or to show to the people at the local fly shop in order to purchase flies that will closely imitate your food samples. Refrigeration of samples is a good, temporary preservation method, or you can use alcohol in glass bottles for more permanent storage.

IDENTIFYING FISH FOODS

All fish foods have distinctive features by which we come to identify them. Many are easy to identify. Actually, the identification of fish, crustaceans, worms, amphibians, reptiles, etc., is usually knowledge most of us already possess. Just from learning experiences that most of us went through in our childhoods, we already know what a frog or a worm looks like. But the principal fish foods of trout and other freshwater fish — insects — are relatively unknown to many of us, and we need some knowledge in order to identify them.

However, insects in their immature and mature forms have distinctive combinations of physical characteristics which make them relatively simple to identify, if you will just take a bit of time to learn how to do it. You should, because identification is critical if you wish to imitate and fish each type of insect upon which the fish are selectively feeding.

I got by for a lot of years using simple suggestive or impressionistic flies, but when I learned about the various important insect groups and how to identify them, my fly-tying skills, my fly-fishing success, and my personal satisfaction really improved. However, in this matter of learning insect identification, *I believe each fly fisherman should be free to advance through the learning process at his own pace!*

IDENTIFYING INSECTS

The body parts of adult and immature insects are the keys to their identification, as shown by the illustration on the opposite page. Each insect group has a unique combination of body parts. The most important parts, from an identification standpoint, are the types of tails, the number and shape of the tails, wingcases or wings, the number and shape of

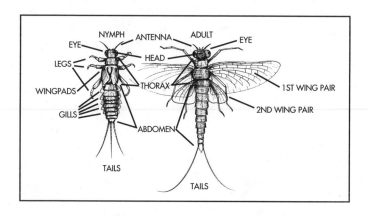

Exterior Parts of the Insect — Nymph and Adult

wings, antennae, gills, and the location of gills or lack of them. But don't let all these anatomical references discourage you. Once you have learned to identify these insects, their overall appearance is usually so apparent that you seldom will have to count tails or check gill locations.

PRINCIPAL FISH FOOD IDENTIFICATION FACTORS

After your initial observation and identification of body parts of an insect (or any other type of fish food), the principal fish food identification factors — the ones that will be of the greatest value to your fishing — are to observe *actions, positions, and movements.* For example, consider how a crayfish *acts,* or how a particular minnow or sculpin *positions itself* in the watery environment, or *which movements* of a grasshopper are tempting the fish to capture and eat it.

OVERLEAF: *Dave Whitlock makes a stillwater presentation on a Montana spring creek slough.*

CHAPTER THREE

CLASSIFICATION AND DESCRIPTION OF THE MAJOR FISH FOODS

There are four major groupings of fish foods: aquatic insects, terrestrial insects, crustaceans, and miscellaneous aquatic life-forms. Of these, insects are by far the most significant fish food form for the freshwater fly fisherman to imitate. They are primarily freshwater fish food sources and are seldom important in the saltwater food chain.

Our modern freshwater fly-fishing methods have their origins in the trial-and-error experiments made by early anglers in Great Britain as they learned how to fish live and artificial insect imitations for their resident trout and grayling. There are two major groups of insects that fish feed on — aquatics and terrestrials.

AQUATIC INSECTS

Aquatic insects are generally the most important to fish because of their year-round availability to fish feeding at the bottom or in various levels of the water column, as aquatic insects spend most of their immature lives beneath the surface as water breathers in streams, lakes, swamps, etc.

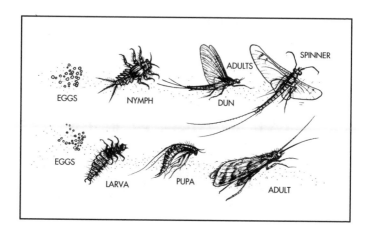

Aquatic Insect Life Cycle Stages — Mayfly (top) *and Caddis* (bottom)

There are also limited periods when they emerge from those waters to transform into air-breathing, sexually mature adults that mate and lay eggs back on those home waters and then die after their mating and egg-laying life-cycle stages have been completed.

In terms of fish foods, there are six major groups of important aquatic insects: mayflies, caddisflies, stoneflies, midges, damselflies, and dragonflies. In addition to these major groups, there are many other miscellaneous aquatic insects, such as water beetles, backswimmers, alderflies, dobsonflies, and fishflies, that fish willingly feed on.

To best imitate and successfully fish these aquatic insects, it is a good idea to be able to identify each type and know some facts about their behavior, preferred environment and life cycle.

Most aquatic insects have either simple egg, nymphal and adult stages; or egg, larval, pupal, and adult stages. The immature stages of the insect, which are its nymphal, larval and pupal life-forms, are water dwelling and breathing. Mature adult forms exist above water as air breathers.

These stages are usually completed in a one-year life cycle, but some insects have two or more generations per year, and others two or four-year life cycles.

In streams, many aquatic invertebrates, especially mayfly nymphs, caddis larvae, stonefly nymphs and midge larvae, make a definite downstream movement. This movement, called "drift," usually occurs soon after dark and just before daylight. These insects actually turn loose of their holds on the bottom and allow the current to move or drift them downstream. There are several probable but unproven explanations for this. Regardless of the reason, opportunistic fish feed significantly on this aquatic invertebrate drift.

If you fish after dark or just before daylight you should take advantage of this feeding by using downstream-drifted nymphal or larval forms.

Many other live foods are also very active after dark or on very dark (cloudy, foggy or stormy) days. The low light intensity gives these creatures some limited safety and thus a sense of security. This is yet another reason why many fish are more active feeders in the low light of dusk and dawn or the darkness of night.

MAYFLIES
Ephemeroptera

Mayflies are a large group of delicate, sail-winged, lovely, harmless, aquatic insects that are probably the best-known hallmark insect to fly fishermen throughout the world. No insect group has received more fly-tying and fly-fishing attention than mayflies. They are most likely the insect that inspired the first development of fly fishing in Europe.

Mayflies occur in most waters that will support an annual population of sport fish. They flourish best in purer water

Life Cycle of a Mayfly — 1. Eggs 2. Nymph 3. Dun 4. Spinner

systems, especially in the watersheds that do not contain a high pH content.

I cannot think of any sport fish, predator or scavenger, that will not eat mayflies where they occur naturally. However, mayfly imitations are most frequently used to catch trout, char, grayling, whitefish and sunfish.

Mayflies have a four-stage life cycle: egg, nymph, dun and spinner. This four-stage cycle begins with the laying of eggs by the spinner female mayfly upon (or just below) the surface of the water. The eggs incubate, develop and hatch into the nymphal stage.

The nymph lives beneath the water for about one year, on the average, until it reaches its mature size. It then makes its way to the water's surface to emerge into the first of its two adult forms, called the *dun* or *subimago*. This sail-winged adult dun then flies to bank cover where it secludes itself to rest and continue its growth. Within minutes, hours or days, it sheds a second skin, transforming itself into its second adult form, the sexually mature *spinner* or *imago*. The spinner joins other spinners to form an airborne mating swarm above or near the water. The spinners mate, the females lay their

Mayfly Nymph Body Types — 1. Swimming 2. Crawling/Clinging 3. Burrowing

eggs on the water, and the females and males soon thereafter die. These emergences vary with species of mayfly, but they usually last from 10 to 20 days or so.

During the intermediate to advanced stages of the nymph, especially during its emergence activity (usually termed "the hatch"), it is the most vulnerable to fish. So this period is usually the most important to fish that are foraging on mayfly nymphs, as the insects are easier to locate and catch for food at that time.

Mayfly Nymph

The mayfly nymph is the immature stage between egg and adult. They are water breathers that dwell mostly on the bottom or burrow below the bottom's surface. A few very mobile species spend part of their time swimming while feeding. In fact, various species of mayfly nymphs have evolved into specific shapes which allow them to live in a variety of watersheds, including still and flowing waters.

OVERLEAF: *A mayfly dun.*

An example of a burrowing-type mayfly nymph.

We identify the nymph of a mayfly by its unique combination of two very small antennae, two distinct wing pads (one pair), visible gills on the upper half of its abdomen, and three long tails.

Most mayfly nymphs have intricate camouflage colors and patterns on the upper sides of their legs and body to match the area in which they live. Their undersides are usually much lighter in color, without much of a camouflage pattern.

When mature, most mayfly nymphs swim to the water's surface, cling to the surface film, and split their back skin lengthwise to emerge into the dun or subimago stage. Some species crawl out on water objects, such as rocks, to hatch.

Mayfly species vary widely in sizes corresponding to hook sizes from #4 to #28, with the most common sizes being #14, #16 and #18.

Dun or Subimago

The mayfly dun, the first of the mayfly's adult forms after its emergence from the nymphal stage, rests on top of the surface just a few seconds or minutes until its wings and body

A natural dun mayfly.

are stabilized or dried. After that it begins to flutter and skate on the surface until it becomes airborne. Once in flight, it heads for waterside plant structures, such as grasses, shrubs, or trees, where it alights and conceals itself to await the further development of its body for the mating function. In most cases this concealment period lasts about 24 to 36 hours, but some duns of the smaller mayfly species can change into their final spinner stage within one or two hours.

Spinner or Imago

The dun sheds a second skin from its body, wings, legs, and tails to transform into the spinner. This transformation produces an adult mayfly that has shiny, more glassy and longer wings, more vivid body colors, and much longer tails and legs — anatomical and cosmetic changes that make the insect more attractive to a mate. Eventually these fully mature mayflies form mid-air mating swarms and mate. The females then return to the water to deposit their egg masses.

A mayfly spinner.

Soon after mating and egg laying occurs, both sexes are exhausted, and they weaken and die.

Fish especially concentrate on these insects as they are staging in their nymphal form on the bottom of the watershed just prior to emergence, during the emergence to the surface, and at the stage when the nymph transforms into the dun. Later, when the male and female spinners fall on the surface to die, there is usually another good feeding opportunity at the surface for these fluttering and dead spinners. When the spent mayfly bodies eventually sink, fish will continue to feed on them at subsurface levels in the water column.

When fly fishing to imitate these specific stages of mayfly development — which is commonly referred to as "matching the hatch" — it is most important to match the size, shape, action and color of the stage on which the fish are concentrating. But it is important to keep in mind that *the fish's feeding activity is seldom static, as fish change their interest preferences quickly as the insects develop from one life-form stage to the other!* So it is not unusual in just a brief period of time to fish four to six types of mayfly imitations to best cover all the feeding opportunities that are presented to the fish by the insects' life-form changes. Incidentally, this is also true with all of the other major aquatic insects that I will discuss.

Adult Mayfly Identification Characteristics (By Stage and Sex)

Dun — The mayfly dun has a single pair of opaquely colored, large sail-shaped wings and a pair of small sail-shaped wings. Its body is long, round and slender and has two or three long tails.

Spinner — The spinner of the insect also has two pairs of wings similar to the dun except that they are longer, more transparent, and more colorful. Its legs, especially the front or first pair, are much longer than that of the dun. And the body is longer than that of the dun, and usually more shiny and colorful. It also has two or three long tails.

Sex — Females are larger by one hook size than males. The males are brighter colored and often different in color than females. The males also have noticeably larger eyes and thinner abdomens.

Fishing Mayfly Imitations

In flowing waters, mayfly nymph imitations are most productive when presented with a natural downstream drift along the bottom, or, during emergence periods, when presented with an action to duplicate a nymph swimming to the surface. The floating nymph or emerged nymph should be presented in the surface film with a natural dead or downstream drift.

In stillwaters, mayfly nymph imitations are most effective if slowly twitched near the bottom when the naturals are not hatching, or twitched and moved slowly from the bottom to the surface when there is a natural emergence of nymphs.

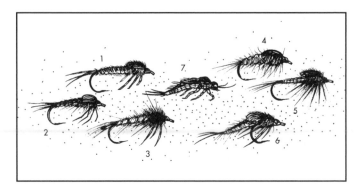

Mayfly Nymph Imitations — 1. Pheasant Tail Nymph 2. AP Series Nymph 3. Whitlock Red Fox Squirrel Nymph 4. Gold-Ribbed Hare's Ear Nymph 5. Red Brown Nymph 6. Swisher/Richards Wiggle Emerger Nymph 7. Natural mayfly nymph

Dun and spinner imitations are usually fished with not much more than a dead or still drift. Sometimes, especially on stillwaters, occasionally twitching them will attract fish strikes better. If it is windy, the naturals will slide across the water surface with the wind. If you see this occurring, try to move your imitation in the same manner.

Mayfly Nymph Imitations
Pheasant Tail Nymph
CDC Nymph Emerger
Gold-Ribbed Hare's Ear Nymph
Red Brown Nymph
Whitlock Red Fox Squirrel Nymph
AP Series Nymph
Swisher/Richards Wiggle Emerger Nymph
Floating-Emerger Nymph
Crippled Emerger
Borger Strip Nymph

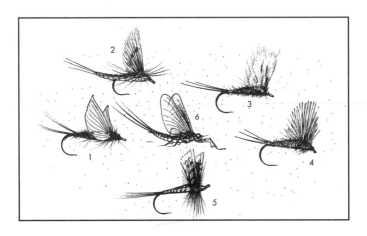

Mayfly Dun Imitations — 1. Swisher/Richards No-Hackle Dun
2. Thorax Dun 3. CDC Dun 4. Comparadun 5. Hackle-
Divided Wing Dun 6. Natural mayfly dun

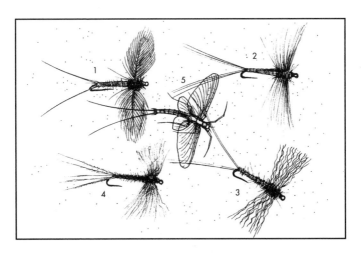

Mayfly Spinner Imitations — 1. Swisher/Richards Hen Spinner
2. Clipped Hackle Wing Spinner 3. Poly-Wing Spinner 4. CDC
Spinner 5. Natural mayfly spinner

Mayfly Dun Imitations
Swisher/Richards No-Hackle Dun — Slow Water
CDC Dun — Slow Water
Comparadun — Slow to Medium Water
Parachute Dun — Medium to Fast Water
Thorax Dun — Slow to Medium Water
Hackle-Divided Wing Dun — Medium to Fast Water
Wulff Hair Wings — Fast to Extra Fast Water

Mayfly Spinner Imitations
Swisher/Richards Hen Spinner
Poly-Wing Spinner
Clipped Hackle Wing Spinner
Crystal Flash Wing Spinner
CDC Spinner

CADDISFLIES
Trichoptera

Caddis or sedges are a large group of aquatic insects that equal or exceed the mayfly as an important fish food. But from man's perspective, they are not nearly as attractive as the mayfly, possibly because in their immature stage they look very much like lowly grub worms, and at their adult stage much like moths.

Apparently it is this less colorful or attractive appearance of caddisflies that makes them less popular for many fly fishermen to attempt to imitate or fish. This is really unfortunate, as on many streams, at many times during the course of the year, caddisflies can be the dominant fish food of trout. And I believe that neglecting the identification or use of them is a serious error in fly-fishing technique.

Caddis have four life-cycle stages, which are the egg, larva, pupa, and adult. Generally, the eggs are deposited by the adult female on the surface of the water. But in some species

Life Cycle of a Caddis — 1. Egg 2. Free Living Larva 3. Cased Larva 4. Pupa Cocoons 5. Emergent Pupa 6. Caddis Adults

the female caddis dives to the bottom and places the eggs on various bottom structures. These eggs soon hatch into larvae.

The larva resembles a grubworm or maggot in appearance. Many species of the caddis larva also build unique cases to conceal and protect themselves from predators.

When the larva reaches its maturity, usually by one year, like the grub or caterpillar of moths and butterflies, most

Examples of caddis cases with the larva exposed.

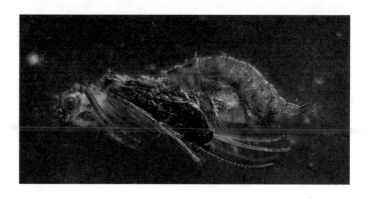

A fully developed caddis pupa ready for emergence.

species of caddis seal themselves into a case or cocoon structure fixed to the bottom of the stream, where they evolve into the pupal form. This is when the transformation from a grub to a more insect-like appearing pupa occurs. When this stage is completed, usually within several weeks, the pupa cuts its way out of the cocoon and rises to the surface or crawls out on a structure above water level. During activity, its pupal skin swells with a gas because of reduced water pressure. It then splits and opens up. The pupa then rapidly emerges from the skin, transforming the insect into a winged, air-breathing adult.

The adult crawls about or skitters across the water's surface as it stabilizes its body and wing formation, then flies away to the nearest terrestrial plant for concealment. After a period of hours of sexual development, adult caddis form into mating swarms in plant cover, and hover over the water to mate and then deposit their eggs either on or in the water, thus completing their life cycle.

An adult caddis commonly lives longer than an adult mayfly, and may make repeated mating flights for periods lasting from several days to as long as a week.

Fish feed daily on free-living caddis larvae and cased larvae along the bottom structures, as well as during their invertebrate drift periods, as I have discussed earlier. However, from the fly fisherman's perspective, the most obvious feeding occurs during the hatch when caddis emerge from their cocoons, swim to the surface, and transform into adults.

You can identify this fish-feeding pattern by hearing and seeing fish make loud, *splashy* surface strikes. As this occurs, you will also see moth-like insects (new adult caddis) flying rapidly away from the surface. If surface feeding occurs and the adult caddis seem to be fluttering above the surface or diving down at it, that is usually a sure indication that the rising fish are feeding on adult mating and egg-depositing caddis.

Caddisflies range in size from 1/8-inch (hook size #24) to 1 1/2 inches long (hook size #4). Most will average between 1/4-inch (hook size #18) to 1/2-inch long (hook size #14).

Caddis pupae and adults are generally easier to imitate than mayflies, because they are more active and erratic in

Free-living green caddis larvae and Dave's imitations of them.

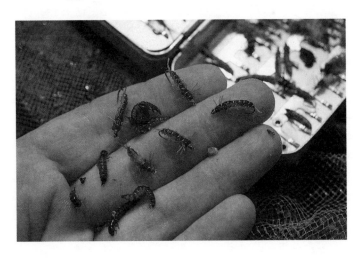

An adult caddis.

their natural movements than mayflies. There are also very few days during the season on most watersheds when there aren't some caddis emerging, laying eggs, or dying on the water. Because of this, caddis-feeding fish are always receptive to caddis imitations, even though there may not be a major caddis hatch or mating swarm occurring.

Caddis Identification Methods

Larva — The bare caddis larva (without case) looks like a grub worm, that is, its head and three thoracic segments with six short legs are more pronouncedly colored than its abdomen. Gills are low on the sides of the abdomen. No antennae or tails are obviously visible.

Cased — You can readily locate the cased caddis by looking for short tubular forms that are made of sand grains, pebbles, or various small bits of aquatic or terrestrial plants which are clinging on surfaces of bottom objects. Pluck these off the bottom and look for the larva's head and legs extending out of the end. You can pull the larva out of its case if you are very careful.

Pupa — Most immature pupae are difficult to locate unless you search the lower sides and underside of bottom structures, for their cocoon-case structures which will be glued tightly to a rock or a log. However, mature pupae can be netted as they emerge upward and swim across the water's surface or crawl out above the water onto a rock or log. The pupa has long legs, tiny wing structures tucked beneath the thorax, and long antennae. There are no visible tail appendages. Usually the abdomen of the pupa is lighter and more brightly colored than its thorax.

Adult — In the air, live adult caddis are very alert, active fliers, and on foot, nervous scramblers. In flight they look similar to a small moth with very long antennae. When positioned on an object, they look moth-like, having a very characteristic tent-shaped, folded-wing outline, with antennae forward or folded over their backs. Their wings are somewhat longer than their bodies. Females have shorter antennae and a thicker and larger profile than males.

Fishing Caddis Imitations

Caddis larva imitations are generally most successfully fished in flowing water. They are best fished with presentations made close or along the bottom with a slow natural drift. Often, in faster water, it is best to use shot or a twist-on weight to keep the imitation next to the bottom.

Caddis pupa imitations work best when sunk near the bottom and then slowly raised with a twitching action towards the surface as the fly drifts downstream. The same procedure is recommended for stillwaters. Many stillwater and some flowing-water caddis pupa emergers rapidly swim up and then across the surface. Pupa imitations fished this way work well during these high-action emergence periods.

OVERLEAF: *Several examples of caddis larvae.*

Caddis Larva Imitations — 1. Dave's Antron Caddis Larva 2. Green Rockworm 3. Anderson Peeking Caddis 4. Harrop Sparkle Case Caddis 5. Natural larva 6. Natural cased larva

Adult caddis imitations are effective with many presentation methods — from dead-drifting to skittering to dappling to diving. It is a good idea to observe what the adult caddis are doing that are causing the fish to respond, and then duplicate that action with your fly.

Caddisfly Imitations
Larva — Green Rockworm
       Harrop Sparkle Case Caddis
       Latex Larva
       Dave's Antron Caddis Larva
       LaFontaine Caddis Larva
       Anderson Peeking Caddis
       Caddis Larva

Pupa — LaFontaine Sparkle Pupa
       Whitlock Red Fox Squirrel Pupa
       Antron Emerger Caddis
       Swisher/Richards Caddis Pupa Emerger

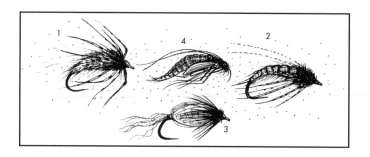

Caddis Pupa Imitations — *1. Swisher/Richards Caddis Pupa Emerger 2. Whitlock Red Fox Squirrel Pupa 3. LaFontaine Sparkle Pupa 4. Natural caddis pupa*

Adult — Borger Poly-Wing Caddis
Troth Elk-Hair Caddis
Henryville Special
Bucktail Caddis
Harrop Partridge Caddis
Buchner Hackle-Wing Caddis
Lawson Spent Partridge Caddis
Goddard Caddis

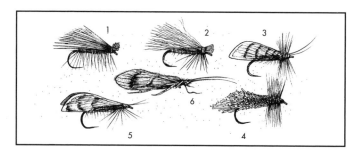

Adult Caddis Imitations — *1. Troth Elk-Hair Caddis 2. Borger Poly-Wing Caddis 3. Buchner Hackle-Wing Caddis 4. Goddard Caddis 5. Harrop Partridge Caddis 6. Natural adult caddis*

STONEFLIES
Plecoptera

Stoneflies are a group of aquatic insects that are widely distributed, especially in high gradient sections of streams. They have a distinctive life cycle and appearance (size and shape) that make it easy for the fish to feed on and fly tyers and fly fishermen to imitate. Most fish will eat them readily.

Most stonefly species have a two to three-year life cycle consisting of three life-form stages: egg, nymphal and adult. The stonefly evolves in a fashion similar to that of the mayfly, but its nymphal stage is longer and its emergence to hatch usually consists of the nymph simply crawling out of the water and onto a shoreline structure. There it splits its nymphal skin and emerges into the winged adult form.

New adults fly or crawl into concealing streamside rock or ledge crevices or terrestrial foliage where they hide, rest and sexually mature. This can take just a few hours or as long as one or two days. Mating occurs in these hideaways. After

Life Cycle of a Stonefly — 1. Adult Laying Eggs 2. Nymphs 3. Emergent Nymph 4. Adult

mating, the females fly back to the water to lay their eggs. Once the eggs are deposited the adults die.

Fish forage on stonefly nymphs year-round, usually taking them off or near the bottom, especially in faster, more shallow sections of a stream or along rocky, windy, shallow lake bottoms. Most nymphs are taken by the fish as they crawl over structures, crawl out to emerge, or during their "invertebrate drift" periods. Because most stonefly nymphs are not strong swimmers, nymph imitations will work most effectively when they are fished *next to the bottom* with a slow, downstream, dead-drift movement — especially in and just below rapids and fast riffles.

Adult stoneflies are another story, for during their emergence they are much less likely to be captured by trout than adult mayflies or adult caddis. When mating and egg laying occurs, however, fish eat them eagerly. Imitations of adult stoneflies can be surface dead-drifted, twitched, and/or skated up, down or across-stream.

Many stonefly emergences and mating/egg-laying flights, especially in the Midwest and East, go undetected by fly fishermen because they occur at night. Adult stoneflies are also frequently fed on during the latter stages of the hatch below the surface as the dead or dying surface-floating adults are submerged by swift, rough, rapid, and riffle waters. During this adult dying period, I very often fish a wet (subsurface) adult stonefly imitation with excellent results.

Stonefly Identification Characteristics

Nymph — At first glance, stonefly nymphs look similar to mayfly nymphs, but are usually larger and have a more distinctive appearance. They have two large antennae, and two distinctive paired wing pads on their thorax. Fuzzy gills

OVERLEAF: *A dark-colored stonefly adult.*

61

are visible only on the lower side and under the thorax segments. There are two very distinctive tail appendages at the end of the abdomen.

Their coloration is usually darker on the top side with intricate camouflage markings, while the underside is much lighter in color. Some nymphs may be much lighter in color, even an off-white or bright yellow. These are nymphs that are going through a skin exchange, or molt period, known as *instar*. Stonefly nymphs are highly vulnerable and attractive to fish at this time because they are softer; much more than when in their normal dark hard-skinned condition. I usually tie some stonefly and mayfly nymph patterns in much lighter shade tones to take advantage of this fish preference for such soft-bodied nymphs.

A stonefly nymph.

A golden-colored adult stonefly.

Adult — The Latin name of the adult stonefly, Plecoptera — meaning folded wings — is derived from the shape of the insect's wings, which at rest lie flat over its body and appear to be rolled or folded together. In flight it has four very long, wide wings and looks as if it were struggling to keep aloft, much like a helicopter out of control. Other than these distinctive wings, adults have a body structure similar in appearance to the nymphs, except they have no gills and are more colorful than the nymphal form.

Stonefly sizes range from 1/2-inch (hook size #16) to 3 inches (hook size #2) in length (including wings). Most stoneflies average about 3/4-inch (hook size #10 to #4) to 2 1/2 inches in length.

Fishing Stonefly Imitations

I believe the most effective way to fish stonefly nymph imitations is in the faster, broken water, and in the riffles and

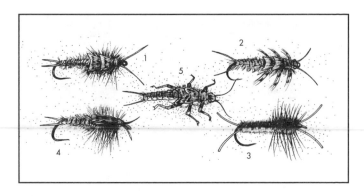

*Stonefly Nymph Imitations — 1. Kaufmann Stonefly Nymph
2. Whitlock Stone Nymph 3. Bitch Creek Nymph 4. Rat-Faced
Krumm Stonefly Nymph 5. Natural stonefly nymph*

runs below them, with a deep, downstream, dead-drifted action. Sometimes slightly twitching the fly a bit as it drifts will encourage strikes.

Adult stonefly imitations are effectively fished when they are dead-drifted, twitched, dappled, or skittered over the water. As the stonefly's hatch and egg-laying activities progress, trout (and bass, too) seem to alter their interest in the natural's actions, and you should adjust the presentation and action of your fly accordingly.

Stonefly Imitations
Nymph — Kaufmann Stonefly Nymph
Whitlock Stone Nymph
Rosborough Stonefly Nymph
Whitlock Red Fox Squirrel Nymph
Borger Mono Stonefly Nymph
Rat-Faced Krumm Stonefly Nymph
Troth Stone Nymph
Bitch Creek Nymph

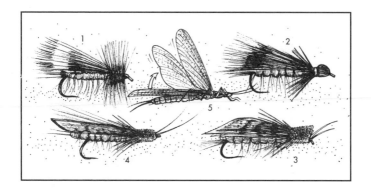

Adult Stonefly Imitations — 1. Sofa Pillow 2. Troth Stonefly
3. Muddler Stonefly 4. Whitlock Adult Stone 5. Natural
adult stonefly

  Adult — Bird Stonefly
              Sofa Pillow
              Improved Sofa Pillow
              Whitlock Adult Stone
              Muddler Stonefly
              Troth Stonefly
              Dave's Hopper

MIDGES
Diptera

As their English name implies, midges are small, two-winged insects that are enormously abundant in most flowing and stillwater fish habitats. Despite their small size, they are a major year-round food source for many species of predator and scavenger fish. Trout, char and panfish feed on them throughout their lives, while other predator fish, such as bass, walleye, and pike, eat midges in their youth.

Because they flourish so well in most freshwaters, midges are an important insect for fly fishermen to imitate. Until

Life Cycle of a Midge — 1. Eggs 2. Larvae 3. Pupation Period 4. Emergent Pupae 5. Adult Emergence 6. Adult

recently, however, midges have not received the respect and attention they deserve. I think this is because they are difficult to imitate, and could not be fished effectively until fly rods, lines, leaders and flies were refined to the point that made imitating midges possible and effective.

Also, it is hard for many fly fishers to appreciate that larger fish — say trout from 16 to 30 inches — will eat mere specks of insects. Perhaps too, man's abhorrence of other blood-sucking forms of this order (Diptera), such as black flies, mosquitos, and deer flies, has assisted in creating a negative image for the harmless midge.

Where trout have grown large and selective under catch-and-release restrictions, midges in sizes #18 to #28 are often the *only* regular reliable way to fool and catch these large fish. And in my opinion, there is no higher plateau of fly fishing than catching big smart trout on 5X to 8X-tippets using #18 to #28 midge imitations with 1, 2, or 3-weight fly rods.

The midge has a life cycle similar to the caddis, that is, four stages which are egg, larval, pupal and adult. They seldom have life cycles longer than one year, and some species have two or more generations per year. Midges hatch year-round in many waters that do not freeze up for extended months.

Midge Identification Characteristics

Larva — The larva of midges is a very simple worm-like stage that has no clearly visible legs, wingcases, antennae or tail appendages. Its body is distinctly segmented and uniform in color over its entire length. Very close inspection of the larva's body with a magnifier will show hair-like structures which are simple gills.

Pupa — The midge pupa has a more detailed body than the larva, with a large head/thorax area and a well-segmented abdomen. Its head and posterior have plume-like gill filaments. Its legs and wingcases are tucked onto the underside of its thorax.

Adult — The adult looks like an adult mosquito. The adult has two distinctive but short wings, six very long legs, a humped thorax, and large plume-like antennae, especially in the male of the species.

An adult midge — note its two small, short wings, long legs and large fluffy antennae.

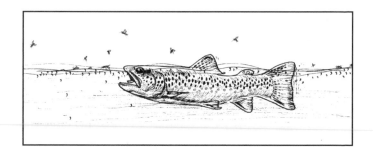

Midge Pupa and Adult Feeding Activity at Surface

Midges have a wide color range, including black, gray, tan, cream, olive, brown, red and purple. They range in size from 1/8-inch (hook size #28) to 5/8-inch (hook sizes #12 or #14). The average size range is from #18 to #22.

Trout Feeding Patterns on Midges

Trout and many other freshwater fish feed on midges year-round with specific feeding patterns. Initially, tiny midge larvae present the first feeding opportunity to the fish. Trout forage for midge larvae when the larvae reach about 1/8-inch (size #28) in length. They eat them more or less in mass as the tiny insects cling to aquatic algae or mosses. Trout will sometimes even eat the host vegetation just to get at the midges and other foods such as snails, scuds, etc.

As the larvae grow larger, fish will eat them more individually, especially during invertebrate diurnal drifts or as the larvae of certain species of midges (Chironomids) come to the surface at night. Also, during fluctuating water levels, common to tailwaters, the larvae may become dislodged from their hiding places and are then taken eagerly by trout.

The pupae are mostly fed upon when they expose themselves as they travel from their fixed cocoons or pupal cases up toward the water's surface. As the pupae concentrate just below or in the surface film, there is much concentrated feeding on them. This is the point where most of the larger midge-feeding trout get serious about capturing and eating midges. They simply cruise about in stillwater, or hold near the surface in flowing streams, and gulp or seine the surface for the emerger midge pupae.

Adult midges are usually most often taken immediately after emergence occurs, while they are resting on the surface or stuck in their shedded pupal skins.

If the hatch is dense enough, these adults will raft or clump together, especially in cold weather, before they lift off in flight. Trout will selectively rise to such a clump when it is available to them. This behavior can frequently be imitated by the fly fisherman through the use of a much larger simulator "clumper" or with the Griffith's Gnat pattern.

Fishing Midge Imitations

Midge larva imitations are best fished on very long, light leaders, and slowly drifted near bottom structures. The use of micro-shot to sink them effectively is recommended, and a strike indicator is a must for the very soft takes.

In both still and flowing waters, pupa imitations are most effectively fished by either slowly pulling them toward the surface or suspending them vertically in the surface film. They are best fished directly to visible, cruising and rising fish.

Adult imitations, fished singly or as a dropper, are most effective when presented directly and precisely downstream, drag-free, to the position of a sighted rising fish. On lakes, adult imitations should be cast well in front of the cruising fish without surface action. The use of two or even three dropper midge adults or pupa combinations for stillwater cruisers is far more effective than fishing just a single fly.

OVERLEAF: *Midges form clumps as they emerge in groups.*

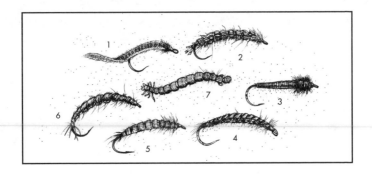

Midge Larva Imitations — 1. Whitlock Chamois Midge Larva
2. Flashabou Midge Larva 3. Brassie Larva 4. Bloodworm
Larva 5. Stalcups Midge Larva 6. Four-Phase Poly Midge
Larva 7. Natural midge larva

Midge Imitations

Larva — Whitlock Chamois Midge Larva
Flashabou Midge Larva
Stalcups Midge Larva
Four-Phase Poly Midge Larva
Bloodworm Larva
Brassie Larva

Pupa — Stalcups CDC Midge Pupa
Smith Palomino Midge Pupa
Four-Phase Poly Midge Pupa
Mathews Serendipity Midge Pupa
Kaufmann Chironomid Emerger
Whitlock Red Fox Squirrel Pupa

Adult — Stalcups CDC Midge Adult
Henryville Special
Conover Midge
Four-Phase Poly Midge Adult

Whitlock Para Midge Adult
Griffith's Gnat
Poly-Winged Midge
Midge Adult Emerger
Smith Palomino Midge Pupa

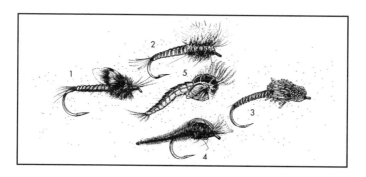

*Midge Pupa Imitations — 1. Kaufmann Chironomid Emerger
2. Stalcups CDC Midge Pupa 3. Mathews Serendipity Midge
Pupa 4. Smith Palomino Midge Pupa 5. Natural midge pupa*

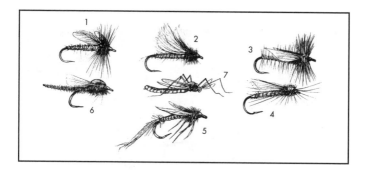

*Adult Midge Imitations — 1. Four-Phase Poly Midge Adult
2. Stalcups CDC Midge Adult 3. Henryville Special 4. Whitlock
Para Midge Adult 5. Midge Adult Emerger 6. Smith Palomino
Midge Adult 7. Natural adult midge*

Diptera

Craneflies are very large, spidery aquatic insects that many fish like to eat. They are widely distributed and abundant in most watersheds. Even though they are Diptera, because of their larger size and life-cycle activities, they are not generally considered to be "midge-like" by fish or fishermen.

Craneflies have a four-stage life cycle: egg, larval, pupal and adult. The larva, which lives along the bottom (or, as it often burrows, several inches beneath it), is a juicy find (3/4-inch to 2 inches in length) for fish. When the larva swims it looks more leech-like than larval in form and shape.

The cranefly pupates out of water along the sides and banks of its home water. When the pupa emerges into the adult, it returns to the water to mate and lay its eggs. Fish often aggressively leap and catch the fluttering, skittering, skating adult on or just above the water. Most of this type action occurs just at sundown and well into darkness. Skat-

A side view of an adult cranefly.

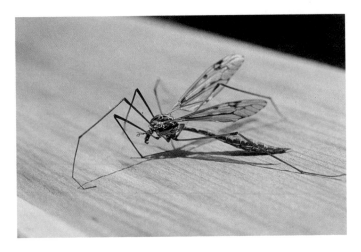

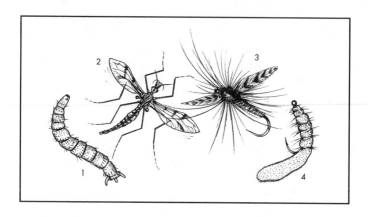

Cranefly Imitations — 1. Natural cranefly larva 2. Natural adult cranefly 3. Whitlock Para Cranefly Adult 4. Whitlock Swimming Chamois Cranefly Larva

ing or twitching large skaters or spider-type dry flies over the water surface is the most effective way to imitate the adults. The larval imitation can be moved through slow or still-waters like a leech. In swift flows, fish your imitation dead-drift with occasional twitching action as it moves deep and downstream.

DAMSELFLIES
Odonata

In their nymphal form, and more especially as adults, dam-selflies and their close relatives, the dragonflies, are aquatic insects that are longer-lived than mayflies, caddis, stoneflies or midges. And since they are very widely distributed in a number of watershed types — cold, cool, warm, slow-flow-ing, and stillwaters, they are a food source for a large variety of predator and scavenger fish.

OVERLEAF: *Male damsel adults hold females as they lay eggs.*

77

Damselfly Pair Depositing Eggs

Damsels are most widely known to anglers who trout fish in cold water lakes and ponds, especially in late spring when the nymphs swim to shore and emerge on aquatic and terrestrial structures. These emergences are also significant in still and slow waters where sunfish, bluegill, bass, and crappie live.

Damsels have a similar life cycle to mayflies and stoneflies, that is, they have only three major life-cycle stages: egg, nymphal, and adult. Their life span averages two to three years.

The damselfly's eggs are uniquely and carefully deposited by the female on floating aquatic plants or similar surface structures just below the water as the male lowers and holds her body while guarding her from predators.

Damselfly nymphs are predacious, active crawlers and swimmers that are often mistaken for small minnows as they swim about. Nymphs live from one to three years before they emerge into the adult form.

Damselfly Identification Characteristics

Nymph — The nymph has three large, distinctive paddle-like tail appendages (these are actually gills). There are no gills or hair-like projections on the abdomen. The abdomen is long and slender, the thorax is short and larger, with long folded wingcases. The nymph's six legs appear to be long and spidery. There are two large eyes on its large head.

Adult — The adult has two equal pairs of long yoke-based wings. There are no visible tails on the abdomen. At rest, the wings are folded and angled up over the insect's back. There are two large eyes. The general appearance of the adult is long, slender, and delicate.

The nymph swims or crawls from offshore to surface-protruding structures such as blooming moss beds, water willows, lily pads, cattails, etc., and then crawls out and hatches into the winged adult. This is a slow process, and the newly emerged adult is weak and pale-colored for several hours before its skin hardens and begins to turn into the color of the mature adult. Its initial flights are often weak or failures.

A live damselfly nymph.

An adult damselfly.

The adult spends several weeks or more feeding on small insects, then mates, after which the female lays eggs and both sexes eventually die.

Fish key in on the adults both when they begin their emergence journey and later as they try their initial flights. But once they are fully capable of flight, flying adults are difficult prey for fish until their mating and egg-depositing activities put them closer to waiting predator fish areas.

Adult damselflies are very beautifully colored and graceful airborne predators. They are always pleasurable to watch while you fish.

Fishing Damselfly Imitations

Damsel nymph imitations are primarily for stillwaters. They work best when cast along the perimeters of aquatic plants with a floating or very slow-sinking fly line with a long leader. Allow the fly to sink about halfway to the bottom, then erratically strip the nymph through the water to imitate the minnow-like swimming motions of the natural. Make frequent pauses of three to 10 seconds.

Adult damsel imitations are most effective during major emergences of the nymph. Present them close to aquatic or terrestrial vegetation sticking out of the water. They should be slightly twitched to simulate the newly emerged adult that has had a hapless first flight failure from the vegetation.

If you notice fish leaping after adults or egg-laying pairs, present the adult imitation to that area as quickly as possible.

Damselfly Imitations
Nymph — Dave's Damsel Nymph
           Dave's New Damsel Nymph
           Borger Marabou Damsel Nymph
           Kaufmann Damsel Nymph
           Jansen Damsel Nymph

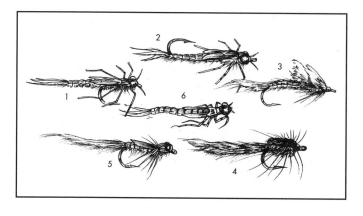

Damselfly Nymph Imitations — 1. Dave's Damsel Nymph
2. Dave's New Damsel Nymph 3. Kaufmann Damsel Nymph
4. Borger Marabou Damsel Nymph 5. Jansen Damsel Nymph
6. Natural damselfly nymph

Adult Damselfly Imitations — 1. Dave's Crystal Damsel
2. Borger Sparkle Wing Damsel 3. Natural adult damselfly

Adult — Dave's Crystal Damsel
        Borger Sparkle Wing Damsel
        Poly-Wing Damsel
        Schroeder Parachute Damsel

DRAGONFLIES
Odonata

Dragonflies are a larger, more robust version of damselflies. They have a similar life cycle, but have more vicious and predacious life habits as nymphs and adults than do damselflies. Because the adults are such active winged hunters of other insect pests, such as black flies, deer flies, mosquitos, moths, etc., they are stocked and used by man for natural control of these pests in agriculture and tourism areas.

Fish, especially larger trout, bass, sunfish, crappie, catfish, perch, and pickerel, really key in on dragonfly nymphs and newly emerged adults. Once dragonfly adults are fully developed, they are much less likely to fall prey to fish because they live and hunt well above and away from their nymphal aquatic homes until egg-depositing time.

Dragonfly Identification Characteristics

Nymph — The dragonfly nymph has six long, spidery legs. It has no visible tail or gills; the gills are inside the nymph's abdomen. An interesting feature on the head is a large labium-mouth device for seizing prey, such as insects, leeches, and small fish. Its two very large eyes are larger than a typical nymph's head. Its long, slender wingcases begin at the thorax and extend half the length of the abdomen.

The dragonfly nymph is a seclusive creature, and moves about with either a spider-like creeping motion, or a jet-speed swimming action created by fast bursts of inhaled water from its rear abdomen intakes — typically in a dart-dart-dart movement pattern. The nymph sizes vary from 1/3-inch to 2 inches in length, with the average being 1 1/4 inches long (hook size #6).

An adult dragonfly at rest on a streamside stick.

Adult — The adult dragonfly has two long, strongly veined pairs of wings clearly separated while in flight or at rest. The forewing is thinner than the rear wings and there are no clearly visible tails or antennae. Its two eyes are very large and its thorax is robust. The abdomen is very long and slender.

Dragonfly sizes vary from 1 3/4 inches to 3 inches in length. Most average about 2 1/2 inches in length, (an extended-bodied pattern in hook sizes #4 or #2).

Most adults are caught by fish as they emerge from their nymphal skins and try to make their first labored test flights. After the adults are mature they are incredibly agile fliers, and are extremely interesting to watch during their hovering, hunting and mating maneuvers. Few fish can leap high and quickly enough to catch these adults.

Fishing Dragonfly Imitations

Dragonfly nymph imitations should be fished in the same method as damselfly nymphs. But since they are larger and more robust, they should be retrieved faster and more aggressively than damselfly nymphs.

Adult dragonfly imitations should also be fished in the style I have recommended for adult damselflies. They work best when nymphs are emerging and during early flight periods before the adult is fully in control.

Dragonfly Imitations
Nymph — Whitlock Dragonfly Nymph #1 and #2
           Kaufmann Lake Dragon
           Kaufmann Floating Dragon Nymph
           Wooly Worm
           Brooks Assam Dragon
           Carney Special

Adult — Whitlock Crystal Dragon
           Betts Foam Dragonfly

Dragonfly Nymph Imitations — 1. Kaufmann Lake Dragon 2. Kaufmann Floating Dragon Nymph 3. Carney Special 4. Whitlock Dragonfly Nymph #2 5. Whitlock Dragonfly Nymph #1 6. Natural dragonfly nymph

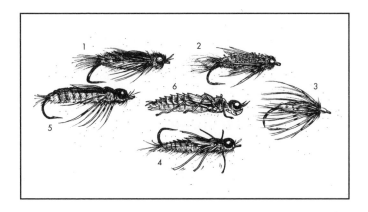

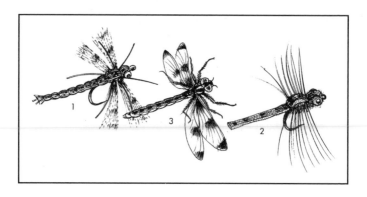

Adult Dragonfly Imitations — 1. Whitlock Crystal Dragon
2. Betts Foam Dragonfly   3. Natural adult dragonfly

ALDERFLIES, DOBSONFLIES, FISHFLIES
Megaloptera

This group of larger aquatic insects is lesser known than the major groups already described, but these insects are highly relished by fish where they are available.

Alderflies, dobsonflies, and fishflies are widely distributed in different watersheds but seldom occur in large numbers as the other major groups I have mentioned. As adults they are mostly nocturnal, which accounts for their lesser popularity with fly fishermen as well as with the fish.

These three Megaloptera have life cycles similar to caddisflies regarding their life-form stages, which are egg, larval, pupal and adult. However, it should be noted that the pupation period occurs on land, not in the ponds, lakes and streams in which the larva thrives.

The larval form is the most significant to imitate, especially if you fish at night in the late spring or early summer. The adults are also worthwhile to imitate, especially for large trout and bass.

The larval imitations of these insects should be fished right next to or rolled over the bottoms of streams in rapids and riffles. To obtain the best results, adult imitations should be twitched and skittered on the surface.

Alderfly, Dobsonfly, and Fishfly Imitations
Nymph — Bailey Braided Hellgrammite Nymph
　　　　　 Whitlock Hellgrammite Nymph

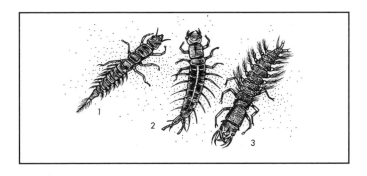

Three Megaloptera Nymphs — 1. Alderfly Nymph 2. Fishfly Nymph 3. Dobsonfly Nymph

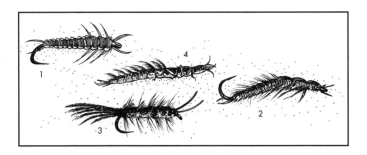

Hellgrammite Nymph Imitations — 1. Bailey Braided Hellgrammite Nymph 2. Whitlock Hellgrammite Nymph 3. Murray Hellgrammite Nymph 4. Natural Hellgrammite Nymph

Murray Hellgrammite Nymph
Black Rubberlegs

Adult — Sofa Pillow
Improved Sofa Pillow
Whitlock Dobsonfly
Muddler Minnow

Adult Dobsonfly, Alderfly, and Fishfly Imitations — 1. Muddler Minnow 2. Whitlock Dobsonfly 3. Sofa Pillow 4. Improved Sofa Pillow 5. Natural adult dobsonfly

BACKSWIMMERS
Hemiptera

These interesting miniature beetle-like insects of slow and stillwater streams, ponds, swamps, and lakes, are widely distributed and sometimes important food sources for trout and various panfish, smallmouth bass, etc.

Backswimmers evolve from egg to nymph to adult in a similar form, gradually developing their adult flight wings as they grow. Most important to the fly fisherman is to recognize them in the waters you fish or in the stomachs of captured fish you examine.

They have distinctive, smooth, tail-less, streamlined beetle shapes with six legs. The third pair of legs is very enlarged

Backswimmers — Top and Side View

and, consequently, creates their characteristic rowing motion through the water column. As adults, they rise, surface, fly and dive back into the water frequently. Fish seem to prefer them best when they are swimming deep in the water column. They are usually quite small in size, from 1/16-inch to 3/4-inch in length (hook sizes #18 to #8).

Dave's Backswimmer Fly

Terrestrial insects are land-born, land-living, primarily air-breathing insects. They become fish food opportunities when they accidently fly over the water, fall on the surface, or sink and drown. The most common land insects that fish regularly eat are ants, beetles, grasshoppers, moths, two-wing flies (bees, wasps), leaf hoppers and spiders (which are not true insects, but are included in this grouping for the sake of convenience).

Most terrestrial insects present surface-film feeding opportunities for fish, but in rough or turbulent water they may sink below the surface. Terrestrials generally are more significant to fish as they increase in size and population, which in the Northern Hemisphere occurs in spring, summer and fall.

Terrestrial insects grow from egg to nymphal or larval forms to adults usually in one year or less. They usually reach their maximum population, size, and activity by mid to late summer, with the activity continuing through autumn. That is usually when they are most important to fish. Because there are so many adult insects competing for food, space and mates, large numbers of terrestrials accidently fall into the water where fish eagerly capture and eat them.

Terrestrial Insects — from left to right: *beetle, ant, hopper, inchworm*

Types of terrestrials number in the thousands, but ants, beetles, grasshoppers and inchworms are the most significant for the angler to imitate, especially for trout, sunfish and bass. These terrestrials are really a favorite food for them.

ANTS
Hymenoptera

Ants are enormously abundant, hourglass-shaped insects that aggressively forage for food constantly from spring thaw through fall freeze up. They are clumsy-footed climbers, and most are unable to fly. Because of this, many fall off grass stems, roots, and tree leaves that extend out over the water where they are quickly consumed by opportunistic fish. Most fish seem to really relish the taste of ants. Therefore, ant patterns are always good flies to use when there is no surface or subsurface hatch activity.

At various times of the year ants form great winged, mating swarms. They seem oblivious to the dangers of water landings and often fall into the water by the hundreds or even thousands. Sometimes a sudden gust of thunderstorm wind will blow down on the water a red or black banquet of flying ants and trigger nearly every trout, sunfish or carp in the water to begin gorging on them. Both wingless and winged

Ant Imitations — 1. Dave's Bright Spot Black Carpenter Ant 2. Foam Ant 3. Natural ant 4. Harrop Flying Ant 5. Fur Ant

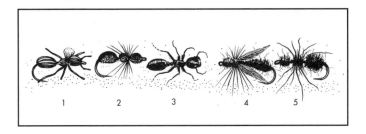

Dave caught this rainbow trout on one of his favorite patterns —
a Bright Spot Black Carpenter Ant.

ants are significant to imitate in sizes ranging from 1/8-inch to 3/4-inch in length. Usually the black ant is the most consistent color to match. My second color choice is an ant pattern of reddish brown.

Imitations are most effective when fished in the surface film, activated by only the natural movement of the water. Ants sink in windy or riffled water, so using wet-fly type ants can also be very effective. Because both small dry and wet ants and beetles are very hard to see on the water, I recommend you use a small (1/8-inch diameter) white or orange wool indicator about six inches from your fly to locate it and assist in detecting strikes.

Ant Imitations
Dave's Bright Spot Black Carpenter Ant
Foam Ant
Harrop Flying Ant
Fur Ant

BEETLES
Coleoptera

Adult beetles are abundant and vary widely in sizes and intricate colors. Most trout seem to prefer the ones that are small (hook sizes #18 to #12), dark, and of simple design. Just as trout seem to key in on the hourglass shape of an ant, they key in on the round shape of the beetle's silhouette when an imitation is fished in the surface film.

Beetle Imitations
Crowe Beetle
Lawson Foam Beetle
Whitlock Elk-Hair Beetle
Dave's Japanese Beetle
Dave's Bright Spot Black Beetle

Beetle Imitations — 1. Crowe Beetle 2. Dave's Bright Spot Black Beetle 3. Natural beetle 4. Lawson Foam Beetle 5. Dave's Japanese Beetle

OVERLEAF: *An assortment of Dave's terrestrial imitations.*

95

GRASSHOPPERS AND CRICKETS
Orthoptera

In my experience, grasshoppers and crickets seem to excite nearly all freshwater predator and scavenger fish. When I used to fish with a cane pole as a kid, grasshoppers and crickets were the only baits I ever used in summer for bass, bluegill, channel catfish, bullhead catfish, crappie, drum and carp. The first really big trout I caught in Montana when I was 16 years old was on a fly rod using a live grasshopper weighted with a split shot.

When grasshoppers, measuring from 1/2-inch to 2 1/2 inches in length, fall into the water kicking and swimming in the surface film, they trigger trout and bass to lose all caution and smash and gobble them! Though they range in colors — olive, brown, black, gray, gold and yellow — the ones that have yellow undersides are usually the most effective to imitate. Small sizes work best early in the season, and larger sizes seem to do better as the season progresses.

Good hopper water is usually lake and stream shorelines that have a lot of weed, grass or low shrub growing right next to and out over the water. Meadow high cut-banks are also

Top view of a live grasshopper on the water's surface. To the left is a Dave's Hopper imitation.

*Grasshopper and Cricket Imitations — 1. Dave's Hopper
2. Lawson Henry's Fork Hopper 3. Dave's Cricket 4. Foam
Rubber Cricket 5. Natural grasshopper 6. Natural cricket*

prime areas. These areas produce best when there is a warm wind gusting off the shore onto the water.

Hopper imitations work best cast down *hard* on the surface close to the shore or bank to imitate a high speed, clumsy hopper's crash-landing downwind. Twitch them to match the hopper's efforts to kick-swim to the shoreline, or let them drift if twitching fails to bring strikes.

Crickets are close relatives of the grasshoppers that often cause feeding frenzies, especially with cool and warm-water fish. For example, crickets are the most favored natural bait for sunfish in the Southeast. They are not always dark brown or black. Many are gray, tan or pale green. Fish the cricket imitations just like you would grasshoppers.

Grasshopper and Cricket Imitations
Dave's Hopper
Joe's Hopper
Lawson Henry's Fork Hopper
Letort Hopper
Dave's Cricket
Foam Rubber Cricket

INCHWORMS
Geometridae

The larvae of moths and butterflies are occasionally abundant enough to be significant fish foods. You'll find in most watersheds that the majority of these larvae fall from the branches or leaves of overhanging shrubs or trees into the water. They are also often eaten as they suspend and hang at the surface from a spider web or drift free on the surface.

The most significant of these "worms" are the so-called inchworm types. These are more or less simple, bare-skinned worms from 3/4-inch to 1 1/4 inches in length, usually in a color of pale green or tan. Simple worm imitations work best if dropped on the surface where you observe inchworms hanging from webs or dead-drifted if you see them drifting downstream. Trout as well as sunfish usually make vigorous, splashy strikes on the natural inchworms, so that is a feeding key you should look for.

Inchworm Imitations
Dave's Bright Spot Inchworm
Deer-Hair Inchworm
Polypropylene Inchworm

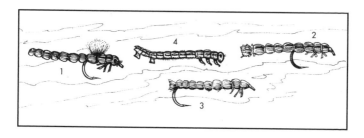

Inchworm Imitations — 1. Dave's Bright Spot Inchworm 2. Deer-Hair Inchworm 3. Polypropylene Inchworm 4. Natural inchworm

CRUSTACEANS

Crustaceans are an extremely and important large live food group for many freshwater fish species. They are widely distributed throughout North and South America, inhabiting all types of waters, but most do best in purer, high alkaline (hard) water with a pH content of 7 or higher. They are usually very easy for predator and scavenger fish to prey upon and have the highest overall food value to fish.

SCUDS
Amphipoda

Scuds, sometimes called freshwater shrimp, are shrimp-like in form and activity. Most species are rather small, from 1/8-inch to 1/2-inch long. They crawl forward over objects, swim forward when foraging, and backwards when fleeing danger. They are simple to imitate, as they have only a simple two-part life cycle, from egg to adult. After they hatch, scuds have the same appearance as they do when mature.

Environment, food, and growth cycles influence the color of scuds, which can range from gray to dark gray, tan, olive, or orange. Scuds (and all other crustaceans) have an exoskeleton or hard skin with pigments and patterns to camouflage them from their predators. In order to grow larger, they seasonally shed this fixed size suit of armor and secrete a larger one to grow into. After shedding the old exoskeleton, they temporarily lose their protective hardness and camouflage which makes them more vulnerable for fish to see, catch and eat. This is called the "soft-shell" condition.

Imitations which suggest or imitate the soft-shell condition are the most effective. The best way to fish them is by moving them slowly and erratically close to structures or

OVERLEAF: *Three examples of the Whitlock Ultrasuede Soft-Shell Crayfish pattern.*

Scud

vegetation on the bottom. In streams, cast the imitation up and across so that it will sink near the bottom. A split-shot or twist-on weight on the tippet may be needed to keep your pattern deep. Mend and drift it downstream with the current at current speed. In stillwater, allow your scud pattern to sink to the bottom, and then, very slowly and erratically, twitch and swim it near the bottom.

Three live scuds in tan, gray, and olive. Color variation is due to the exoskeleton "skin" change phase; gray is the hard shell, olive is the just-forming skin, and tan is the soft-shell condition.

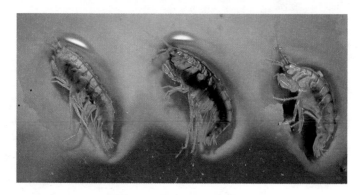

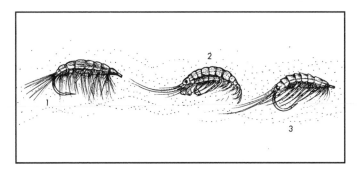

Scud Imitations — 1. Kaufmann Scud 2. Natural scud 3. Whitlock Scud

Scud Imitations
Kaufmann Scud
Whitlock Scud
Gold-Ribbed Hare's Ear Nymph
Whitlock Red Fox Squirrel Nymph
Bighorn Fluorescent Scud

SOWBUGS
Isopoda

Sowbugs (sometimes called cressbugs) are close relatives of the scuds and, in fact, often inhabit the same watersheds. Different types of fish such as trout, panfish, minnows, and scavenger fish love to eat sowbugs.

Sowbugs are quite similar in appearance to scuds, but they can readily be distinguished by the fact that their bodies are much more horizontally flattened, and their legs protrude from the sides of their bodies, whereas the legs of scuds protrude from their undersides. Also, they do not swim as well as scuds, and are only able to crawl over underwater objects. The bodies of most sowbugs are from 1/16-inch to 3/8-inch long, and are usually speckled gray in color. They

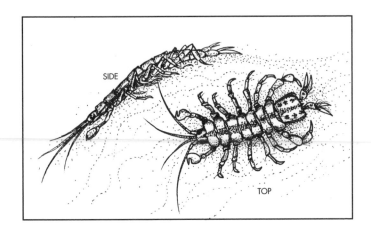

Sowbug — Side and Top View

actually strongly resemble the terrestrial bugs that as kids we called "roly-poly" or "pill" bugs.

Since they are not good swimmers, they are most difficult to imitate in stillwaters. To be effectively fished in streams, they must be precisely dead-drifted with the current near the

Sowbug Imitations — 1. Dave's Sowbug 2. Whitlock Red Fox Squirrel Nymph 3. Cressbug 4. Gold-Ribbed Hare's Ear Nymph 5. Natural sowbug

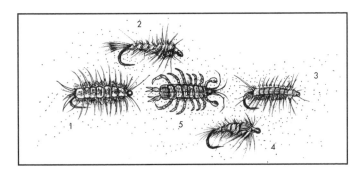

bottom. Present them to visible foraging fish, and use a very sensitive strike indicator system to detect the slow, soft takes fish use when eating the natural sowbugs in a stream.

Sowbug Imitations
Dave's Sowbug
Cressbug
Brown's Sowbug
Whitlock Red Fox Squirrel Nymph
Gold-Ribbed Hare's Ear Nymph

CRAYFISH
Decapoda

Crayfish (sometimes called crawfish or mud bugs) are, in my opinion, at the top of the fish food groups as a most important natural food that fish prefer, especially larger fish. They are widely distributed and relatively easy for predator and scavenger fish to find and catch in both still and flowing waters. *I believe that fish prefer crayfish over any other foods.*

Like scuds, crayfish are camouflaged by a variety of color patterns that help them conceal themselves in their environment. In their soft-shell stage they lose their somber, more natural colors (brown and olive) and become somewhat lighter and brighter, sometimes even turning a fluorescent orange. Crayfish are commonly 1/2-inch to 3 inches long, but sometimes reach 5 to 6 inches in length.

They are mostly nocturnal, preferring to hide beneath or in bottom structures and aquatic vegetation during daylight hours. At sunset, they crawl about outside these hideouts and become scavengers searching for live and dead foods. This is the time when they become most vulnerable to attacks by fish. If the attack is more than they can defend themselves against with their two strong, sharp, pinching claws, crayfish will swim backwards with a thrusting motion from their tails to escape danger. This backward swimming motion, which consists of a series of fast darts over the bottom and back to the cover and safety of rock crevices or moss beds, is the unique characteristic of the crayfish that fly fishermen should attempt to imitate.

Therefore, crayfish patterns that are heavily weighted in their tail section and tied to swim in a backward position are the most effective imitations — especially if they are also soft in texture to simulate the soft-shell condition fish prefer.

Cast the crayfish imitation to the area you wish to fish over, let it sink and rest on the bottom for a short while, and then quickly and erratically dart/swim it off, over, and up from the bottom to a height of three or four feet in the water

Note the color difference of these crayfish; the reddish orange is in the soft-shell condition which fish much prefer to eat.

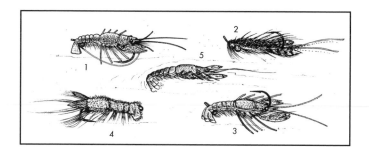

Crayfish Imitations — 1. Joe Robinson Mud Bug 2. Whitlock Near Nuff Crayfish 3. Whitlock Ultrasuede Soft-Shell Crayfish 4. Clouser Crayfish 5. Natural crayfish

column. At that point stop the retrieve, let the pattern drift down again, and repeat the backward panic-swimming motion. In streams, you can simply allow the crayfish to drift downstream and drag it over the bottom as an alternate method of simulating the backward panic-swimming action.

Crayfish Imitations
Joe Robinson Mud Bug
Whitlock Near Nuff Crayfish
Whitlock Ultrasuede Soft-Shell Crayfish
Clouser Crayfish

MISCELLANEOUS AQUATIC LIFE-FORMS

FORAGE FISH

Most predator fish and many scavenger fish regularly eat other smaller fish, even those of their own species. In the early 1940s and 1950s, brown trout were often labeled cannibals by cold-water fishery biologists, thus fostering a bad reputation for the brown in comparison to other trout. The

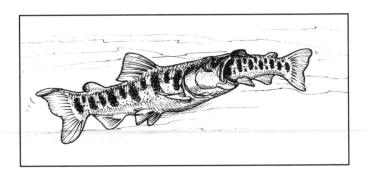

Trout Parr Eating a Trout Fry

situation became so bad that in some states, biologists removed wild browns by shocking and poisoning them.

In fact, *all predator fish are cannibals,* and they usually prefer to eat other fish if they can be easily captured. I once ran a series of trout, salmon and char egg-hatching experimental observations, hatching over 500 rainbow, brown and brook trout, steelhead, Atlantic salmon, Chinook salmon and silver salmon. I placed all the eggs in gravel in a large cold water aquarium. These eggs hatched within weeks of each other, and the fry were fed all the tiny live shrimps they wanted. Yet just days out of the gravel all these different species of trout, char and salmon were eating their own kind and any others they could catch! Within six weeks only about 50 parr Chinook salmon, out of the original 500 fish of different species, existed in the aquarium.

Minnows such as chub, dace, shiners, smelt, sculpin, etc., will eat the fry of trout, bass, pike, sunfish, salmon, and even their own eggs. But, in turn, these different types of minnows can soon become forage themselves as some of their former prey survive and grow to a size large enough to swallow them! You might say that it is a "fish-eat-fish" watery, cannibalistic society in the waters we fish.

Forage Fish — from left to right: *shad, dace, and sculpin*

Forage fish have a two-stage life cycle of egg and fish, and tend to congregate in similarly sized schools or small groups. Matching the size of these is usually a good idea for better results with selectively feeding larger fish.

To simplify the differences among forage fish for fly imitating and fishing purposes, I like to categorize them into three basic groups according to their environmental activity and their availability as prey for gamefish. All these forage fish are imitated by relatively large streamer patterns. Sizes in 1/2-inch increments from 1 inch to 3 1/2 inches long are the most effective for most gamefish. However, I recommend that you have a few 4 to 8-inch long forage fish imitations if you wish to tempt the largest browns, bass, pike and musky.

Group I

These are open-water, schooling fish, especially in deep stillwater areas or larger rivers. Usually, they are deep-sided, narrow-backed, more or less silvery fish. Typical examples are shad, shiners, alewife, smelt, ciscos and herring.

OVERLEAF: *Whitlock Match the Minnow Yellow Perch patterns.*

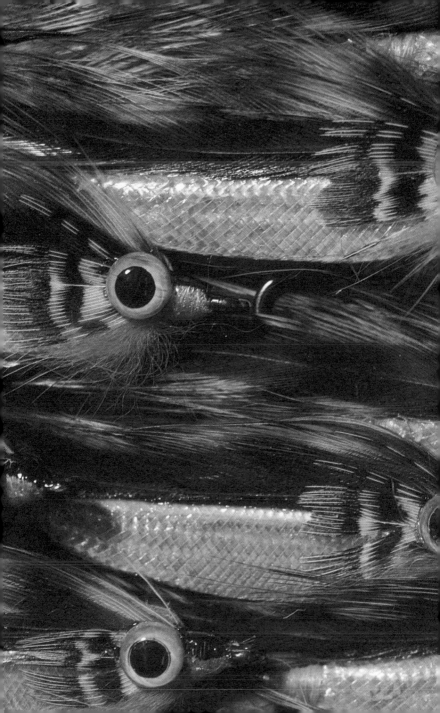

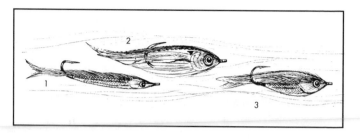

Group I Forage Fish Imitations — 1. Whitlock Match the Minnow Smelt 2. Whitlock Sheep Shad 3. Whitlock Match the Minnow Shiner

Group I Forage Fish Imitations

Whitlock Sheep Streamer (Imitates shad, alewife, shiners and smelt.)

Whitlock Match the Minnow Streamer (Imitates shad, alewife, golden shiners, and smelt.)

Gray Ghost Streamer

Group I imitations are usually most effective in lakes and large, slow rivers when trout, stripers, landlocked salmon,

Group II Forage Fish Imitations — 1. Whitlock Match the Minnow Stickleback 2. Matuka Spruce 3. Match the Minnow Yellow Perch 4. Zonker 5. Match the Minnow Black Nose Dace

Examples of the Whitlock Match the Minnow Lake Smelt.

bass, white bass, walleye etc., are chasing and attacking large schools of forage fish at the surface, along shallow shorelines, or off long points.

Group II

These are shallow-water, loosely schooling, long, oval-bodied fish with strong lateral line color markings to blend with the color of the water and structures of their environment. Typical examples are chub, dace, sticklebacks, trout, shiners, yellow perch, eels and fall fish.

Group II Forage Fish Imitations

Whitlock Match the Minnow Streamer (Imitates stickleback, black nose dace, perch and trout parr.)
Black Nose Dace Bucktail
Muddler Minnow
Matuka Spruce (in silver, gold, brown and olive)
Zonker

Group II imitations are most effective in lakes and streams fished near the surface or just off the bottom where trout, bass, pike, and walleye etc., ambush them from near shoreline structures, rocky runs and riffles, and around beds of aquatic vegetation.

Group III

These are bottom-dwelling, compressed and flat-bodied fish with intricate back and side color camouflage markings. They have a chameleon-like ability to alter the intensity of their existing color, or change colors entirely, as they swim near or rest on the bottom. Typical examples from this group are sculpin, darters, catfish, suckers, and lamphries. Salamanders, though not forage fish, are also effectively imitated by this group's imitative flies.

Group III Forage Fish Imitations

Whitlock Matuka Sculpin
Spuddler
Muddler Minnow

Group III Forage Fish Imitations — 1. Troth Bullhead 2. Whitlock Matuka Sculpin 3. Spuddler 4. Whitlock Hare Sculpin 5. Whitlock Near Nuff Sculpin 6. Muddler Minnow

Natural sculpins and Dave's Matuka Sculpin imitations.

Whitlock Hare Sculpin
Troth Bullhead
Whitlock Near Nuff Sculpin
Whitlock Hare Water Pup

Group III imitations are most effective when cast against the shoreline and darted straight out into the deeper water or fished with a dead-drifted or erratic motion right along the bottom of lakes and streams.

These three groups of forage fish should be imitated with streamer flies that are designed to look like them. But just as important, their position in the water, and the swimming action you impart to them, must emulate the live naturals. I suggest having forage fish streamer imitations that either float on the surface, sink slowly, or sink very rapidly, so that you have the capability of presenting one anywhere in the water column that forage fish might be located. It is also very important to make your imitations look alive and attractive and vulnerable to a predator fish looking for an easy meal. I accomplish this by giving my streamers action that will imitate a forage fish that is either injured, feeding without care, in panic, or dying.

FISH EGGS

Many predator and scavenger fish love to eat their own eggs, as well as those of other species, especially those of trout, char, and salmon in the larger egg sizes (3 mm to 7 1/2 mm). Sucker, carp, and catfish egg clumps are also highly prized as food by many scavenger and predator fish.

You should fish egg imitations in the spawning areas where the natural eggs have been deposited, slowly and close or on the bottom. The only natural movement eggs have is the movement imparted to them by the flow of water.

However, you should take care — *please!* — not to disturb the spawning fish with your egg-imitation fly fishing. It is not

Fish Egg Imitations — 1. Yarn Fly   2. Roe Bug   3. Glo-Bug 4. Whitlock Double-Egg Sperm Fly   5. Lee Krystal Egg 6. Sucker Egg Cluster   7. Natural trout eggs   8. Natural sucker eggs   9. Natural salmon eggs

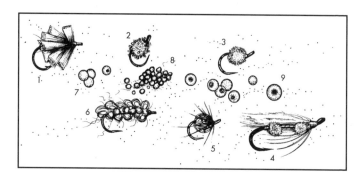

a sportsmanlike thing to do, and can destroy the spawn of our valuable wild fish.

Fish Egg Imitations
Glo-Bug
Single Egg Fly
Sucker Egg Cluster
Whitlock Double-Egg Sperm Fly
Roe Bug
Lee Krystal Egg
Yarn Fly

LEECHES
Hirudinae

To most humans, leeches are no more than slimy, blood-sucking, watery vampires; but to many fish they are a highly desirable dinner. Many fly fishermen feel the leech is one of the best fish foods to imitate to consistently catch larger trout, bass, or walleye, especially in slow or stillwater fisheries. I agree.

Leeches range in size from 1 to 6 inches in length, but 2 to 3 inches seems to be the most effective length for a leech

Swimming Leech

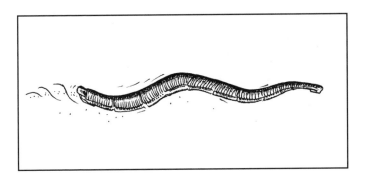

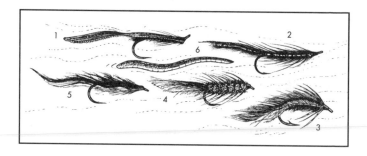

Leech Imitations — 1. Whitlock Chamois Leech 2. Whitlock Lectric Leech 3. Borger Gray Strip Leech 4. Woolly Bugger 5. Marabou Leech 6. Natural leech

imitation. Most leeches have colors similar to the water and bottoms they live on, usually olive, brown, gray, or mottled black and olive. They swim with their entire bodies in a smooth, slow, up-and-down motion that is easy to imitate with a leech fly weighted in the head area.

Imitations of leeches are most effective when fished at intermediate to near-bottom depth. With a floating line and long leader, or a slow-sinking line and short leader, allow the leech pattern to sink to the desired depth. Then begin a slow, short, strip/pause . . . slow, short, strip/pause type of retrieve. This works best in slow or stillwater. For fast water, just let your fly sink and drift along with the current.

Leech Imitations
Marabou Leech
Whitlock Lectric Leech
Borger Gray Strip Leech
Woolly Bugger
Whitlock Chamois Leech

The best moment after a strike of a big trout. ➤

AQUATIC WORMS
Annelida

Aquatic worms are very similar in appearance to the earth or manure worms which kids dig up to fish for sunfish, but are normally smaller, about 3/4-inch to 1 1/2 inches in length, and a bit brighter in color.

They live on the bottoms of many streams and are consistently eaten by trout and other fish that you would normally expect to catch on earthworms. They are easy to sample and observe with a small seine and some digging.

Fly fishermen, naturally being prejudiced against using worms as bait, generally ignored the importance of aquatic worms as a fish food until the San Juan Worm was popularized on the San Juan River and other western trout rivers. Now that pattern is used all over the country by nymph fishermen with good success.

The aquatic worm isn't a true swimmer, but it does become dislodged by water fluctuations or streambed distur-

A Bighorn brown caught on a San Juan Worm.

Aquatic Worm Imitations — 1. San Juan Worm 2. Whitlock Chamois Worm 3. Plastic Worm 4. Ultra Chenille Worm 5. Natural aquatic worm

bances and will drift and tumble along with the current. So imitations are most effective when fished right on or very near the bottom with a natural drift. For consistent results, it is best to use a split-shot or twist-on weight to keep the worm at its most effective depths.

> *Aquatic Worm Imitations*
> San Juan Worm
> Whitlock Chamois Worm
> Plastic Worm
> Ultra Chenille Worm

OVERLEAF: *Emily Whitlock had the right imitation to take this trophy New Zealand brown.*

CHAPTER FOUR

DAVE'S TACKLE TIPS

Many books in a fisherman's library understandably cover the important subject of fly-fishing tackle in great detail. But to get in my two cents on the subject, I think it's worth a little space in this book to emphasize a few basic tackle principles. Keep in mind that after you have successfully identified and tied on what you believe to be an effective imitative fly, you need a tackle system that allows you and your fly-fishing skills to put the imitation exactly where the natural foods are being taken by the fish. In other words, your line and leader must position your fly *precisely and realistically* where the fish will feel most tempted to eat it. You may also need to give action to your imitation, by manipulating it with your rod, line, and leader to give it the appearance of live food. If you do this well you will have excellent results. And of course, if you don't, you won't.

The fly rod should be chosen according to which rod casts the imitations correctly. Usually the smallest flies, #16 to #24, are best for casting at short to intermediate distances, say, from 15 to 40 feet. Rods with slow to medium actions, and fly line weights from 1 to 5, are ideal for such small-fly casting and fishing.

For larger flies, #14 to #4, with a requirement to cast in the 20 to 60-foot range, rods with medium to fast action and fly line weights from 6 to 8 are ideal.

With the very largest flies, say, from #4 to #5/0, with a requirement to cast from 25 to 80 feet, best performance will be achieved with the powerful fast-action fly rods and fly line weights from 8 to 12.

The rod length must be chosen by considering the distance of the cast you will be making and how restricted the area is you must do this in. Generally, 7 to 8-foot rods work best for short casts in restricted or brush areas, while 8 1/2 to 10-foot rods work best for more open areas and longer casts.

Rod length is also important for controlling the fly line, leader and fly as they are "fished," i.e., mending, twitching, animating, etc. Longer rods from 8 1/2 to 10 feet in length make the best line/fly control fishing tools.

Fly lines are the weight that pulls the fly to the target and that keeps you in control of the fly's position on the water. The various tapered floating fly lines are the most useful to position flies on the surface or as deep as three or four feet in the water column with optimum control.

Sinking-tip and full-sinking fly lines are more effective in sinking and holding flies at greater depth in the water column, say from three to 20 feet, particularly in stillwater. But remember, the more of the line length that sinks down into the water column, the more sensitivity and fly control you lose. That's a compromise you'll have to make, however, to fish most imitations in deeper waters.

The leader is extremely important, even critical, to the success of making the imitation look and act real. Generally, the leader's purpose is to provide a link of low visibility and high flexibility between the higher visible, stiffer fly line and the fly. Its design should:

1. Aid in accurate, deceptive fly presentation from the cast.
2. Help float or sink the fly to the water position you want it to move into.

3. Allow the fly to move in a lifelike manner, as unencumbered as a natural food would be.
4. Have strength enough to resist breaking when either you or the fish strike or pull hard on it. And act like a stretchy shock absorber as the fish swims against the force you are applying while fighting (tiring) the fish.

In my opinion, well-designed knotless, tapered, co-polymer nylon leaders are superior to level, knotted tapers or braided tapered leaders. For example, in my work with Umpqua Feather Merchants we have been able to design and manufacture special-purpose knotless tapered leaders, such as our Midge-Nymph, Spring Creek, Bass, Salmon, and Sinking Line models, that do amazingly good jobs of "fishing" flies correctly. *The leader is the key to allowing the fly to fish realistically!*

Even knotless tapered leaders can be improved or repaired by the addition of more tippet material with a blood knot or double surgeon's knot to increase the leader length and reduce tip diameters as the fishing circumstances require.

When I am trying to precisely imitate very small foods, say hook sizes #16 to #28, I lengthen my tip with supple tippet material as much as 24 to 48 inches. In comparison to a short leader tip, this added tippet significantly improves the performance of the fly to give it natural floating, drifting, sinking, or swimming action.

INDEX

(Featured imitative patterns appear in boldface)